# The Influence of Internal Barriers on Open Innovation

Despite providing us with a good understanding of how firms use certain mechanisms to benefit from open innovation strategies, current research provides only limited insights into how barriers internal to the firm may hamper knowledge transfer and limit effective utilization of external knowledge sources.

*The Influence of Internal Barriers on Open Innovation* proposes a dynamic perspective that addresses this gap and aims at stimulating this discussion in two ways. First, by looking at how the way firms structure their internal (innovation) activities may (unintentionally) create barriers to the incorporation of external knowledge. Second, by reflecting on how internal barriers might be coupled to firm decisions aimed at the optimization of innovation processes, like the balance between exploration and exploitation strategies.

The chapters of this book provide detailed conceptualization and investigation of organizational characteristics and practices that influence internal barriers to open innovation. The diverse set of studies described in the chapters of this book will help open innovation scholars to better understand the challenges that firms face when dealing with internal barriers that affect their external knowledge search and knowledge sourcing.

The chapters in this book were originally published as a special issue of the journal *Industry and Innovation.*

**Pedro de Faria** is Professor of Innovation Management at the University of Groningen (the Netherlands). His research has appeared in journals such as the *Journal of Management, Journal of International Business Studies* and *Research Policy.*

**Florian Noseleit** is Associate Professor of Entrepreneurship and Innovation at the University of Groningen (the Netherlands). His research has been published in journals like *Strategic Management Journal, Journal of Management* and *Journal of Regional Science.*

**Bart Los** is Professor of the Economics of Technological Progress and Structural Change at the University of Groningen (the Netherlands). He published innovation-related research in journals like *Research Policy, Journal of Evolutionary Economics* and *Regional Studies.*

# The Influence of Internal Barriers on Open Innovation

*Edited by*
**Pedro de Faria, Florian Noseleit and Bart Los**

Routledge
Taylor & Francis Group
LONDON AND NEW YORK

First published 2021
by Routledge
2 Park Square, Milton Park, Abingdon, Oxon, OX14 4RN

and by Routledge
52 Vanderbilt Avenue, New York, NY 10017

*Routledge is an imprint of the Taylor & Francis Group, an informa business*



*British Library Cataloguing-in-Publication Data*
A catalogue record for this book is available from the British Library

ISBN13: 978-0-367-70475-9 (hbk)
ISBN13: 978-1-003-14655-1 (ebk)

Typeset in Minion Pro
by codeMantra

**Publisher's Note**
The publisher accepts responsibility for any inconsistencies that may have arisen during the conversion of this book from journal articles to book chapters, namely the inclusion of journal terminology.

# Contents


*Citation Information* vi

*Notes on Contributors* vii

Introduction: The influence of internal barriers on open innovation 1
*Pedro de Faria, Florian Noseleit and Bart Los*

1 What facilitates external knowledge utilisation in SMEs? – An optimal configuration between openness intensity and organisational moderators 6
*Nan Kyung Kim and Joon Mo Ahn*

2 Internal barriers to innovation and university-industry cooperation among technology-based SMEs in Brazil 31
*Diego R. De Moraes Silva, Luis Otávio Lucas and Nicholas S. Vonortas*

3 Harnessing adaptive capacity to close the pandora's box of open innovation 60
*Maral Mahdad, Chiara Eleonora De Marco, Andrea Piccaluga and Alberto Di Minin*

4 Collaborative ties and ambidextrous innovation: insights from internal and external knowledge acquisition 81
*Xuemei Xie, Yanru Gao, Zhipeng Zang and Xiaohua Meng*

*Index* 107

# Citation Information

The chapters in this book were originally published in the *Industry and Innovation*, volume 27, issue 3 (March 2020). When citing this material, please use the original page numbering for each article, as follows:

**Introduction**

*The influence of internal barriers on open innovation*
Pedro de Faria, Florian Noseleit and Bart Los
*Industry and Innovation*, volume 27, issue 3 (March 2020) pp. 205–209

**Chapter 1**

*What facilitates external knowledge utilisation in SMEs? – An optimal configuration between openness intensity and organisational moderators*
Nan Kyung Kim and Joon Mo Ahn
*Industry and Innovation*, volume 27, issue 3 (March 2020) pp. 210–234

**Chapter 2**

*Internal barriers to innovation and university-industry cooperation among technology-based SMEs in Brazil*
Diego R. De Moraes Silva, Luis Otávio Lucas and Nicholas S. Vonortas
*Industry and Innovation*, volume 27, issue 3 (March 2020) pp. 235–263

**Chapter 3**

*Harnessing adaptive capacity to close the pandora's box of open innovation*
Maral Mahdad, Chiara Eleonora De Marco, Andrea Piccaluga and Alberto Di Minin
*Industry and Innovation*, volume 27, issue 3 (March 2020) pp. 264–284

**Chapter 4**

*Collaborative ties and ambidextrous innovation: insights from internal and external knowledge acquisition*
Xuemei Xie, Yanru Gao, Zhipeng Zang and Xiaohua Meng
*Industry and Innovation*, volume 27, issue 3 (March 2020) pp. 285–310

# Contributors

**Joon Mo Ahn** Graduate School of MOT (Management of Technology), Sogang University, Seoul, South Korea.
Institute for Manufacturing, University of Cambridge, UK.

**Pedro de Faria** Department of Innovation Management & Strategy, University of Groningen, the Netherlands.

**Chiara Eleonora De Marco** UC Berkeley, USA.
Institute of Management and Department EMbeDS/DEXRAI – Scuola Superiore Sant'Anna, Pisa, Italy.

**Diego R. De Moraes Silva** Department of Science and Technology Policy, University of Campinas, Brazil.

**Alberto Di Minin** Institute of Management, Scuola Superiore Sant'Anna, Pisa, Italy.

**Yanru Gao** School of Management, Shanghai University, China.

**Nan Kyung Kim** Graduate School of MOT (Management of Technology), Sogang University, Seoul, South Korea.

**Bart Los** Department of Global Economics & Management, University of Groningen, the Netherlands.

**Luis Otávio Lucas** Department of Science and Technology Policy, University of Campinas, Brazil.

**Maral Mahdad** Department of Social Sciences, Wageningen University, the Netherlands.

**Xiaohua Meng** School of Politics and Public Administration, Soochow University, Suzhou, China.

**Florian Noseleit** Department of Innovation Management & Strategy, University of Groningen, the Netherlands.

**Andrea Piccaluga** Institute of Management, Scuola Superiore Sant'Anna, Pisa, Italy.

**Nicholas S. Vonortas** Department of Science and Technology Policy, University of Campinas, Brazil.
Institute for International Science and Technology Policy & Department of Economics, The George Washington University, Washington, DC, USA.

Institute for Statistical Studies and Economics of Knowledge, National Research University Higher School of Economics, Moscow, Russia.

**Xuemei Xie** School of Management, Shanghai University, China.

**Zhipeng Zang** School of Communication, East China University of Political Science and Law, Shanghai, China.

 OPEN ACCESS

# The influence of internal barriers on open innovation

Pedro de Faria, Florian Noseleit and Bart Los

## 1. Introduction

Firms increasingly rely on alliances, joint ventures and other collaboration agreements to develop their innovation activities (Bogers et al. 2017). The evidence that accessing external knowledge sources has enabled many firms to improve their performance (Lahiri and Narayanan 2013; Laursen and Salter 2006; Sampson 2007) paved the way towards an open innovation paradigm. However, evidence also shows us that the benefits from external knowledge sources vary considerably across firms. This heterogeneity is explained by the fact that the value that firms can draw from external knowledge is not only dependent on external and contextual factors, but also on a variety of internal, firm-specific factors. In fact, various studies document substantial heterogeneity in the abilities of firms to reap the benefits from external knowledge sources (e.g. Cassiman and Veugelers 2006; Kale and Singh 2007; Keil et al. 2008; Lahiri and Narayanan 2013; Rothaermel and Deeds 2006). In particular, these studies have given attention to particular investment and strategic decisions that firms make in order to improve their capabilities to internalise external knowledge. Examples are the creation of dedicated alliances departments or other less formalised mechanisms aimed at stimulating interdependencies between external and internal technology investments (Antonelli and Colombelli 2015; Heimeriks, Duysters and Vanhaverbeke, 2007; Noseleit and de Faria 2013; Wuyts and Dutta 2014) and the strategic use of knowledge protection mechanisms, like patents and secrecy (Hannah 2005; James, Leiblein, and Lu 2013; Sofka, de Faria, and Shehu 2018).

Despite providing us with a good understanding of how firms use certain mechanisms to benefit from open innovation strategies, current research provides only limited insights into how barriers internal to the firm may hamper knowledge transfer and limit effective utilisation of external knowledge sources. While a considerable body of research addresses a broad array of internal barriers to knowledge dissemination (e.g. Karim 2009; Karim and Kaul 2014; Tortoriello, Reagans, and McEvily 2011; Tsai 2001), this work is only partially integrated in the literature on open innovation and external knowledge sourcing (e.g., Keil et al. 2008; Lahiri and Narayanan 2013; Faems et al. 2019).

## 2. Overview of the special issue

This special issue aims at reflecting on how internal barriers may affect open innovation and external knowledge search processes. By identifying the resistance of internal actors to external knowledge as an important internal barrier to external knowledge integration, the literature addressing the not-invented-here syndrome (Clagett 1967; Katz and Allen 1982; Agrawal, Cockburn, and Rosell 2010) already provide us essential insights on how internal barriers might hamper the integration of external knowledge. Despite acknowledging its relevance, we claim that this literature provides only an incomplete picture, since internal barriers are not limited to not-invented-here syndrome related processes. That is, there is a need for a more detailed conceptualisation and investigation of organisational characteristics and practices that may act as internal barriers to external knowledge sourcing. With this special issue we want to stimulate this discussion in two ways. First, by looking at how the way firms structure their internal (innovation) activities may (unintentionally) create barriers to the incorporation of external knowledge. Second, by reflecting on how internal barriers might be coupled to firm decisions aimed at the optimisation of innovation processes, like the balance between exploration and exploitation strategies. We are confident that the diverse set of papers that constitutes this special issue contributes to these discussions.

In the first paper of this special issue, Kim and Ahn (2019) use the open innovation framework to investigate how particular organisational dimensions influence a firm's ability to take advantage of external knowledge. They build on the assumption that firms, in order to effectively make use of external knowledge, need to adapt their traditional innovation routines and incorporate openness in their innovation processes. More specifically, the authors address how the implementation of knowledge management, incentive systems and knowledge appropriation mechanisms are linked to the open innovation processes of Korean SMEs. The results show that systematic knowledge management is an essential facilitator of external knowledge integration and that entrepreneurial orientation – despite being undervalued by SMEs – also plays an important role in open innovation processes. Moreover, they find that the optimal configuration of mechanisms is dependent on the degree of openness, a result that highlights the need to question the implementation of 'one size fits all' open innovation strategies for SMEs.

Moraes Silva, Lucas, and Vonortas (2019), in the second paper of this special issue, take a different viewpoint on how organisational dimensions of SMEs are interrelated with external knowledge sourcing. They investigate how internal innovation barriers influence the decision of SMEs to search for external knowledge via collaboration agreements with universities and research institutes. The results provide evidence that both, the perception of financial and knowledge obstacles, lead firms to rely on universities and research institutes for their innovation activities. These findings highlight the idea that internal barriers not only influence the success of innovation activities directly, but may also impact the way SMEs structure their innovation activities and search for external knowledge.

In the third paper of this special issue, Mahdad et al. (2019) look at the stage that follows a firm's decision to collaborate with universities and investigate how firms adapt their activities to this particular type of open innovation activity. By means of a case study focused on the cooperation activities between an Italian telecommunication company and five universities, the authors investigate how the firm deploys adaptive capacities to address the challenges associated to the organisational and cultural changes driven by open innovation. The results suggest that multiplexity of relationships can help organisations to build trust and optimise their interactions with partners that are organisationally and culturally distant. Moreover, they find that task redundancy and loose coupling facilitate collaboration and, consequently, knowledge sharing. This study brings new insights to our understanding of how organisations adapt to collaboration activities and optimise their use of external knowledge.

Finally, in the paper that closes this special issue, Xie et al. (2019) investigate how collaboration influences the degree to which a sample of Chinese firms is able to effectively combine explorative and exploitative innovation activities. They find that the positive effect of collaboration on ambidextrous innovation is driven to a larger extent by internal knowledge acquisition than by external knowledge acquisition. This study highlights how internal knowledge processes play a crucial role on the utilisation of knowledge from external parties and how innovation performance is heavily dependent on how firms balance internal and external processes.

In sum, the four studies that constitute this special issue bring us four complementary perspectives on collaboration and open innovation processes. They stress the challenges that firms face when dealing with collaboration partners and help us reflect on how internal barriers and processes are deeply interconnected with external knowledge acquisition. What is more, they reflect on how collaboration might, on the one hand, be a source of additional resources that help firms' to develop innovation activities but, on the other hand, might also bring additional challenges that require organisational adaptation.

## 3. Open innovation and internal barriers: a need for a dynamic perspective

West, Vanhaverbeke, and Chesbrough (2006) and more recently Salter, Criscuolo, and Ter Wal (2014) have stressed the need to expand our understanding of how open innovation is often hampered by internal barriers. This special issue contributes to this debate by highlighting the dynamic nature of the challenges that firms face when dealing with internal barriers that affect their external knowledge search and knowledge sourcing. Moreover, this reflection allows us to propose some interesting avenues for future research relating open innovation to internal barriers. First, the papers in this special issue give indication that organisations are heterogeneous in the degree to which they face internal barriers and how they deal with those barriers. We believe that future open innovation studies should explore this heterogeneity since it can have important consequences for external knowledge sourcing. In particular, it is important to understand how organisational structural factors and management practices influence the way firms define internal knowledge processes that might generate and mitigate internal barriers to external knowledge sourcing. Second, besides organisational level factors, the type of knowledge that is exchanged with external parties might also influence how internal barriers affect open innovation processes. Therefore, we encourage researchers to explore how the effect of internal barriers on knowledge sourcing varies with the cognitive and technological distance between external knowledge and the internal knowledge base of a firm. Moreover, future studies should also investigate which organisational strategies allow firms to deal effectively with internal barriers in cognitive and technological diverse contexts. Third, while existing research has been able to identify what may constitute internal barriers to open innovation, there is still limited understanding of the mechanisms linking these barriers to external knowledge acquisition and utilisation. In particular, future studies should investigate how internal barriers guide knowledge search and influence sorting and matching processes of collaboration partners. In sum, we believe that this collection of papers has moved the discussion further and provides a good basis for scholars to advance our knowledge on how intra-organisational barriers influence external knowledge utilisation in open innovation settings.

## References


Agrawal, A., I. Cockburn, and C. Rosell. 2010. "Not Invented Here? Innovation in Company Towns." *Journal of Urban Economics* 67 (1): 78–89. doi:10.1016/j.jue.2009.10.004.

Antonelli, C., and A. Colombelli. 2015. "External and Internal Knowledge in the Knowledge Generation Function." *Industry and Innovation* 22 (4): 273–298. doi:10.1080/13662716.2015.1049864.

Bogers, M., A. K. Zobel, A. Afuah, E. Almirall, S. Brunswicker, L. Dahlander, … J. Hagedoorn. 2017. "The Open Innovation Research Landscape: Established Perspectives and Emerging Themes across Different Levels of Analysis." *Industry and Innovation* 24 (1): 8–40. doi:10.1080/13662716.2016.1240068.

Cassiman, B., and R. Veugelers. 2006. "In Search of Complementarity in Innovation Strategy: Internal R&D and External Knowledge Acquisition." *Management Science* 52 (1): 68–82. doi:10.1287/mnsc.1050.0470.

Clagett, R. P. 1967. "Receptivity to Innovation – Overcoming N.I.H." Master Thesis, MIT.

Faems, D., B. Bos, F. Noseleit, and B. Leten. 2019. "Multistep Knowledge Transfer in Multinational Corporation Networks: When Do Subsidiaries Benefit from Unconnected Sister Alliances?" *Journal of Management* in press. doi:10.1177/0149206318798037.

Hannah, D. R. 2005. "Should I Keep a Secret? the Effects of Trade Secret Protection Procedures on Employees' Obligations to Protect Trade Secrets." *Organization Science* 16 (1): 71–84. doi:10.1287/orsc.1040.0113.

Heimeriks, K. H., G. Duysters, and W. Vanhaverbeke. 2007. "Learning Mechanisms and Differential Performance in Alliance Portfolios." *Strategic Organization* 5 (4): 373–408. doi:10.1177/1476127007083347.

James, S. D., M. J. Leiblein, and S. Lu. 2013. "How Firms Capture Value from Their Innovations." *Journal of Management* 39 (5): 1123–1155. doi:10.1177/0149206313488211.

Kale, P., and H. Singh. 2007. "Building Firm Capabilities through Learning: The Role of the Alliance Learning Process in Alliance Capability and Firm-level Alliance Success." *Strategic Management Journal* 28 (10): 981–1000. doi:10.1002/(ISSN)1097-0266.

Karim, S. 2009. "Business Unit Reorganization and Innovation in New Product Markets." *Management Science* 55 (7): 1237–1254. doi:10.1287/mnsc.1090.1017.

Karim, S., and A. Kaul. 2014. "Structural Recombination and Innovation: Unlocking Intraorganizational Knowledge Synergy through Structural Change." *Organization Science* 26 (2): 439–455. doi:10.1287/orsc.2014.0952.

Katz, R., and T. J. Allen. 1982. "Investigating the Not-invented-here (NIH) Syndrome: A Look at the Performance, Tenure and Communication Patterns of 50 R&D Project Groups." *R&D Management* 12 (1): 7–19. doi:10.1111/j.1467-9310.1982.tb00478.x.

Keil, T., M. Maula, H. Schildt, and S. A. Zahra. 2008. "The Effects of Governance Modes and Relatedness of External Business Development Activities on Innovative Performance." *Strategic Management Journal* 29 (8): 895–907. doi:10.1002/smj.672.

Kim, N. K., and J. M. Ahn. 2019. "What Facilitates External Knowledge Utilisation in SMEs? an Optimal Configuration between Openness Intensity and Organisational Moderators." *Industry and Innovation* forthcoming. 1–25. doi:10.1080/13662716.2019.1632694.

Lahiri, N., and S. Narayanan. 2013. "Vertical Integration, Innovation, and Alliance Portfolio Size: Implications for Firm Performance." *Strategic Management Journal* 34 (9): 1042–1064. doi:10.1002/smj.2013.34.issue-9.

Laursen, K., and A. J. Salter. 2006. "Open for Innovation: The Role of Openness in Explaining Innovative Performance among UK Manufacturing Firms." *Strategic Management Journal* 27 (2): 131–150. doi:10.1002/smj.507.

Mahdad, M., C. E. De Marco, A. Piccaluga, and A. Di Minin. 2019. "Harnessing Adaptive Capacity to Close the Pandora's Box of Open Innovation." *Industry and Innovation* forthcoming. 1–21. doi:10.1080/13662716.2019.1633910.

Moraes Silva, D. R. D., L. O. Lucas, and N. S. Vonortas. 2019. "Internal Barriers to Innovation and University-industry Cooperation among Technology-based SMEs in Brazil." *Industry and Innovation* forthcoming. 1–29. doi:10.1080/13662716.2019.1576507.

Noseleit, F., and P. de Faria. 2013. "Complementarities of Internal R&D and Alliances with Different Partner Types." *Journal of Business Research* 66 (10): 2000–2006. doi:10.1016/j.jbusres.2013.02.025.

Rothaermel, F. T., and D. L. Deeds. 2006. "Alliance Type, Alliance Experience and Alliance Management Capability in High-technology Ventures." *Journal of Business Venturing* 21 (4): 429–460. doi:10.1016/j.jbusvent.2005.02.006.

Salter, A., P. Criscuolo, and A. L. Ter Wal. 2014. "Coping with Open Innovation: Responding to the Challenges of External Engagement in R&D." *California Management Review* 56 (2): 77–94. doi:10.1525/cmr.2014.56.2.77.

Sampson, R. C. 2007. "R&D Alliances and Firm Performance: The Impact of Technological Diversity and Alliance Organization on Innovation." *Academy of Management Journal* 50 (2): 364–386. doi:10.5465/amj.2007.24634443.

Sofka, W., P. de Faria, and E. Shehu. 2018. "Protecting Knowledge: How Legal Requirements to Reveal Information Affect the Importance of Secrecy." *Research Policy* 47 (3): 558–572. doi:10.1016/j.respol.2018.01.016.

Tortoriello, M., R. Reagans, and B. McEvily. 2011. "Bridging the Knowledge Gap: The Influence of Strong Ties, Network Cohesion and Network Range on the Transfer of Knowledge between Organizational Units." *Organization Science* 23 (4): 1024–1039. doi:10.1287/orsc.1110.0688.

Tsai, W. 2001. "Knowledge Transfer in Intraorganizational Networks: Effects of Network Position and Absorptive Capacity on Business Unit Innovation and Performance." *Academy of Management Journal* 44 (5): 996–1004.

West, J., W. Vanhaverbeke, and H. Chesbrough 2006. "Open Innovation: A Research Agenda." *Open innovation: Researching a new paradigm*. 285–307.

Wuyts, S., and S. Dutta. 2014. "Benefiting from Alliance Portfolio Diversity: The Role of past Internal Knowledge Creation Strategy." *Journal of Management* 40 (6): 1653–1674. doi:10.1177/0149206312442339.

Xie, X., Y. Gao, Z. Zang, and X. Meng. 2019. "Collaborative Ties and Ambidextrous Innovation: Insights from Internal and External Knowledge Acquisition." *Industry and Innovation* forthcoming. 1–26. doi:10.1080/13662716.2019.1633909.

# What facilitates external knowledge utilisation in SMEs? – An optimal configuration between openness intensity and organisational moderators

Nan Kyung Kim and Joon Mo Ahn

**ABSTRACT**

This study explores the complex relationships between open innovation (OI) climate and OI activities by investigating the changing moderating effects of organisational facilitators in small innovative firms. Our partial least squares structural equation modelling analysis suggests (1) OI-friendly climate promotes OI activities, (2) this process is further facilitated by various organisational efforts, but (3) the efforts firms must put in are proportional to the level of openness intensity. The findings also suggest that systematic knowledge management is the most basic facilitator, while entrepreneurial orientation is generally underperformed despite its high importance. This study provides implications for managers and policymakers who lead OI adoption and implementation.

**Abbreviation:** SMEs - Small and Medium-sized Enterprises; PLS-SEM - Partial Least Squares - Structural Equation Modeling

## 1. Introduction

Open innovation (OI) has received increasing attention over the 15 years (West et al. 2014b; Bogers et al. 2017). To date, its advantages have been extensively researched, and many case studies of successful OI in various types of firms and industries have been reported (Vanhaverbeke, Chesbrough, and West 2014; Ahn et al. 2019). Yet, admittedly, not all firms succeed in OI adoption and implementation (Deichmann, Rozentale, and Barnhoorn 2017). OI implementation is a laborious task for large established firms (Zynga et al. 2018), and these implementational challenges would be more critical in small and medium-sized enterprises (SMEs), which lack resources. Although there are some lessons and implications from large established firms, those are not directly transferred to SMEs with different organisational characteristics (Vanhaverbeke et al. 2018). Large firms can even conduct parallel innovation experiments by launching an internal and external innovation project simultaneously (Minshall et al. 2010), but SMEs may have to find the optimised best route to cope with their resource constraint. However, while many studies have investigated whether openness can result in performance enhancement (e.g., Mazzola, Bruccoleri, and

Perrone 2012; Ahn, Minshall, and Mortara 2015), few studies have considered 'the process that leads to OI' (Huizingh 2011).

OI distinguishes itself from traditional-closed innovation in that it allows the utilisation of external knowledge, demands relationship coordination, and requires the establishment of a new innovation routine. This complex nature and various practical challenges in its implementation have made it more difficult for SMEs to employ it. OI involves substantial changes in organisation, such as new task set-ups and job function transitions (Salter, Criscuolo, and Ter Wal 2014). Therefore, the successful implementation of OI depends on how well a firm can facilitate openness by changing its operational configuration. As noted by Zynga et al. (2018), firms' distinctive organisational routine and their structural setting can explain why not all firms successfully implement OI. Many studies have focused on the outputs (e.g. financial performance or the number of new products) from openness rather than its process, but OI is a complicated journey that requires substantial new resource investment and re-allocation (Chiaroni, Chiesa, and Frattini 2011; Zynga et al. 2018). Although many case studies have showed the positive side of OI, the behind-the-scenes situation is not pretty. Despite the potential benefits openness may provide, a journey to OI would be very challenging for SMEs. Owing to their insufficient resources, SMEs must find an optimal organisational setting to maximise the benefits from openness.

In this regard, this study suggests a more integrative view to illustrate the complex OI mechanism – what organisational configuration can facilitate OI in SMEs? The current research investigates various types of OI activities (from a wide range of external search to in-depth collaboration) and attempts to identify the best optimised configurations for each OI activity by examining the moderation effects of knowledge management, incentive system, and knowledge appropriation. To this end, data from 389 innovative SMEs from the manufacturing sector are analysed using the partial least squares (PLS) structural equation modelling (SEM) method. PLS-SEM is chosen because it is effective for explorative studies and more robust to non-normality; moreover, it provides useful additional information, such as for importance–performance map analysis (IPMA) (Ringle and Sarstedt 2016).

Our results suggest that organisational facilitators moderate the OI climate-OI activity relationship which varies according to the intensity of openness. More organisational facilitators are required for OI activities with a higher degree of openness, suggesting that the organisational efforts firms must put in are proportional to the level of openness intensity. Also, the results show that systematic knowledge management is the most basic facilitator, while entrepreneurial orientation is generally underperformed despite its high importance. These findings suggest that firms, particularly SMEs that may lack resources needed to engage in OI successfully, must first decide what OI activity they will conduct, and find an optimal fit between organisational efforts and intensity of OI activities.

This paper comprises five sections. The theoretical background is illustrated in the next section, followed by an explanation of the data and methodology. Then, the results are presented. The paper concludes with the implications and limitations of this study.

## 2. Theoretical background

The resource-based view (RBV) considers a firm as an entity consisting of bundles of idiosyncratic resources (Barney 1991), and it has been used to explain why a firm gains its competitive advantages. In the literature, RBV has been an important theoretical pillar for studies analysing the impacts of a firm's internal resources on performance (Mowery, Oxley, and Silverman 1998; Galende and De La Fuente 2003). However, recent studies on RBV have extended its boundary to the strategic utilisation of external resources, because firms, particularly SMEs, attempt to establish a relationship with external entities to acquire the necessary resources they lack (Tether 2002; Kang and Park 2012). By opening their boundaries, SMEs can utilise external resources for their internal innovation, and in this process, they can even lower risks and uncertainty by sharing them with external partners or networks. Some studies have suggested that SMEs can achieve greater benefits from openness than larger firms because of their organisational advantages, such as simple hierarchy, ability to change, and swift adaptation to different environments (i.e. flexibility). Yet, admittedly, the factor of scarce resources plays a dual role in SMEs. It motivates SMEs to expand their boundaries but simultaneously hinders smooth utilisation of external resources. Substantial absorptive capacity is required to understand and integrate external knowledge (Cohen and Levinthal 1990), and intellectual property management would be more challenging (Laursen and Salter 2014). Moreover, they are typically more vulnerable to knowledge leakage (Oakey 2013). Also, change management is not simple. In an OI paradigm, newness and heterogeneity are imported from outside organisations, which demand firms to establish a different innovation routine. In this respect, SMEs must establish an OI-friendly atmosphere to minimise internal resistance and optimise their organisational settings to maximise the benefits of OI activities they are implementing. Because OI is a complex activity with various degrees of openness and SMEs cannot simultaneously invest in every type of innovation activity (Dahlander and Gann 2010; Ahn, Minshall, and Mortara 2015), it is imperative for them to distinguish what settings are necessary for high-level openness and what configuration is suitable for low-level openness.

## 2.1. Organisational settings facilitating openness

In the traditional closed process of innovation, necessary knowledge is created within firms, so every innovation stage is controlled and managed internally. Yet, because OI is the process of innovating innovation (Chesbrough 2003), its adoption demands that firms deviate from the current routine and impose new job roles/functions on employees (Salter, Criscuolo, and Ter Wal 2014). Firms should also be able to manage the uncertainty embedded in external knowledge and relationships (Oakey 2013). In this regard, firms must be ready for change and embrace heterogeneity from openness.

OI climate is a vital prerequisite for the adoption and implementation of open approaches (Remneland Wikhamn 2011; Kratzer, Meissner, and Roud 2017). Hung and Chiang (2010) defined OI climate as strategic proclivity for conducting OI activities. Damanpour (1991) suggested that the success of innovation is a function of organisational characteristics, such as organisational atmosphere and structure. OI demands significant operational transformation and redefinition of the current tasks and boundaries (Foss, Laursen, and Pedersen 2011; Salter, Criscuolo, and Ter Wal 2014), but this transition cannot be initiated without a positive evaluation of openness. The attitude towards an object can represent the degree of intention to act in accordance with a variety of behaviours with respect to that object (Fishbein and Ajzen 1975). In this respect, a high level of OI proclivity, which is affected by a high level of organisational flexibility and entrepreneurial orientation (EO), will lead firms to actively leverage external knowledge, and we suggest that OI climate plays an important role in OI implementation process.

OI-friendly climate is a sufficient condition that shows good potential for OI, but it is not a necessary condition. As not all individuals with a good physical condition succeed as athletes, the organisational atmosphere will not always guarantee successful OI. If OI-friendly climate plays a leading indicator role, making firms unfreeze and ready to move, the 'configuration of organisational settings' will be an important facilitator accelerating the OI process from moving to institutionalising. OI climate may be referred to an organisational trait or an innate disposition, and this sufficient condition can be further stimulated/promoted by numerous organisational settings (Kratzer, Meissner, and Roud 2017). This study examines the moderation effects of various facilitators – knowledge management, incentive system, and knowledge appropriation strategy. These organisational settings are selected to reflect the complicated characteristics of OI and the various challenges embedded in it.

First, knowledge management will play an important role in OI. The essence of OI lies in the utilisation of external knowledge, but this exploration may remain ineffective if the ability to exploit external knowledge internally is not established (Martini, Neirotti, and Appio 2017). Access to various external information sources cannot simply be equated with intensive utilisation of external knowledge. Absorptive capacity is required to understand and digest new external knowledge (Cohen and Levinthal 1990; Spithoven, Clarysse, and Knockaert 2011; West and Bogers 2014a), and to achieve this, a systematic knowledge management process must be established to reallocate and refine new external information (Ahn et al. 2016; West and Bogers 2014a; Zobel 2017). Because OI stresses knowledge flow via a firm's permeable boundary, one of the core competences in OI is well-structured knowledge management and orchestration. To create new value and ensure synergy from openness, knowledge match-making must be conducted successfully; to achieve this, some employees or sub organisations must keep track of and systematically maintain the knowledge flow. This is a process of differentiating gems from pebbles. Since not all external information contributes to the creation of new value, systematic gate-keeping, tracing, and filtering of knowledge input will play a vital role in promoting OI activities.

Second, incentive setting can encourage employees to be more actively involved in external search and collaboration. OI imposes different missions and goals on internal members (Salter, Criscuolo, and Ter Wal 2014), so it will be important for firms to motivate and stimulate employees' change momentum. Because of the extroverted nature of OI, firms must transform their innovation process substantially. Yet, not all the transition goes smoothly. Employees may agree with the necessity of this transformation, but they may not like losing control of an internal R&D project. Although employees acknowledge that external knowledge is better than internal one, some may hesitate or at least not voluntarily engage in external knowledge exploration. Therefore, an incentive system is necessary to overcome such difficulties (Felin and Zenger 2014; Popa, Soto-Acosta, and Martinez-Conesa 2017). Such a system is adopted to prevent possible 'agency problems' and align the interests of the firm with those of its employees

(Fu 2012). An appropriate reward system will provide the necessary motivation for employees to pay greater attention to external resources and mitigate their negative attitudes towards external knowledge. As noted by Fu (2012), incentives are positively associated with innovation efficiency, which suggests that challenges individuals face in OI can be effectively addressed through an incentive system.

Third, a knowledge appropriation strategy will promote OI. Although openness provides many economic advantages, firms must find an optimal balance between openness and closedness (West 2003; Laursen and Salter 2014; Zobel, Lokshin, and Hagedoorn 2017). To achieve successful collaboration, firms must, to some extent, share key information to obtain partners' trust and commitment; however, such knowledge sharing can threaten firms' technology confidentiality and even threaten monopoly profits (Bianchi et al. 2011; Laursen and Salter 2014; Oakey 2013). Thus, to cope with this challenge, firms must establish a knowledge protection strategy, and various approaches should be explored – not only formal (i.e. patents, trademarks, and copyrights) but also informal (i.e. lead-time advantages, complex design, and secrecy) tools can be used. These knowledge protection tools play a safeguarding role by protecting the necessary core assets while releasing relatively unnecessary knowledge on the shelves (Chesbrough 2003). As suggested by Di Minin, Frattini, and Piccaluga (2010) in their case study of *Fiat*, setting an appropriation strategy would be one of the important initial steps for a high level of openness.

### 2.2. Openness intensity and organisational facilitators

Because OI is a multifaceted concept embracing various characteristics (Spithoven, Vanhaverbeke, and Roijakkers 2013), the effect of organisational facilitators (e.g., knowledge management, incentive and knowledge appropriation) can vary according to the intensity of openness. Laursen and Salter (2006) proposed the concepts of search 'breadth' and 'depth', which are, in fact, not identical in terms of their focus and openness intensity. Search breadth asks how many external information sources are searched for innovation, thus stressing quantity. Because breadth measures the number of information targets, it is highly likely that a broad search remains explorative, shallow, and superficial (Cruz-González et al. 2015). In contrast, search depth asks how importantly each information source is used, so a deep search attempts to measure intensive and repetitive knowledge exploitation and puts more emphasis on quality. Therefore, compared with the shallow broad search, considerably more effort will be required for deep search.

A similar logic can be applied to the difference between search and collaboration. Unlike search in which external information is unilaterally imported, collaboration is a two-way process demanding interactive understanding, adaptive trust building, and stronger engagement (Ahn, Minshall, and Mortara 2018). Search only handles passive knowledge content, but innovation collaboration deals with both knowledge and active knowledge creators. Thus, as noted by Zahra and George (2002) and Zobel (2017), various additional capacities, such as relational capacity, will be necessary for collaboration to create and maintain an interactive partnership positive and constructive. In this regard, as shown in Figure 1, it is suggested that the intensity/degree of openness increases from breadth to depth and from search to collaboration.

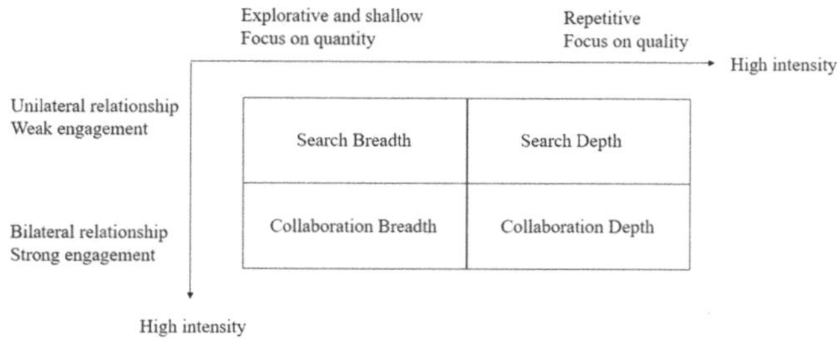


**Figure 1.** Intensity of openness.

Therefore, considering this complexity of openness, it is postulated that 'further considerable organisational effort (i.e. more implementational settings) will be necessary for the promotion of highly intensive OI activities. Organisational factors, such as knowledge appropriation, have been an important tool for maintaining core competence (Teece 1986), but as noted by Laursen and Salter (2014) and Holgersson, Granstrand, and Bogers (2018), the role of such factor has been developed in more complex ways in an OI paradigm. Formal appropriation, such as intellectual property (IP) licensing, demands time and costs for its implementation, so it might not effectively moderate the relationship between OI climate and every type of OI activity, particularly in SMEs lacking resources. Moreover, firms must recognise that collaboration is not the same as knowledge search. External search is a unilateral activity, in that knowledge can be obtained from even free information sources, such as conferences and academic articles. However, in collaboration, utilising this kind of knowledge may not demand a strong agreement or a relationship-building process. Therefore, less organisational factors moderate the linkage between OI climate and OI activities, while more organisational factors are necessary to strengthen the influence of OI climate on the complicated form of openness, such as intensive and repetitive collaboration engagement. Hence, we suggest the following hypotheses:

*Hypothesis: The likelihood that organisational facilitators (e.g., knowledge management, incentive and knowledge appropriation strategy) moderate the OI climate-OI activity relationship varies according to the intensity of openness.*

## 3. Data and methods

### *3.1. Measurements*

#### *3.1.1. Open innovation climate*

OI climate is a vital prerequisite for OI (Remneland Wikhamn 2011; Kratzer, Meissner, and Roud 2017). When considering the complex characteristics of OI, it is highly likely that OI-friendly atmosphere is influenced by a firm's behavioural tendency – how well it embraces newness and take the necessary risks. In this vein, OI climate is affected by organisational flexibility and EO (entrepreneurial orientation). For the analysis, based on the work of Hung and Chiang (2010), eight items were used to measure the latent variable – OI climate (Climate). All factors were measured using a 7-point Likert scale ranging from 1 (strongly disagree) to 7 (strongly agree). Some indicators were dropped after the first confirmatory factor analysis, as shown in Table 1. Five out of eight OI climate items were significantly loaded on the construct with loading values larger than 0.61 (p-value < 0.001). Organisational flexibility (FLEX) represents the ways in which decision delegation and multiple communication channels are linked and geared towards achieving high levels of organisational performance (Laursen and Foss 2003; Foss, Laursen, and Pedersen 2011). OI demands that firms embrace newness to establish a new innovation routine, so they must adopt a flexible attitude towards change to benefit from this newness. This pragmatic attitude will contribute to increasing the intensity of change momentum. Organisational flexibility which was originally suggested by Khandwalla (1977) and further developed by Naman and Slevin (1993), was used. Nine items were utilised to assess this variable; one item (FLEX06) was deleted owing to its lack of loading value in the confirmatory factor analysis. After the second confirmatory factor

**Table 1.** Measurement model.

| Construct | Indicator | Factor loading | Internal consistency | Convergent validity | Discriminant validity | Reference |
|---|---|---|---|---|---|---|
| Organisational flexibility (FLEX) | FLEX01 | 0.76*** | Cronbach's alpha = 0.897 rho_A = 0.869 | AVE = 0.5 C.R = 0.887 | Accepted | Khandwalla (1977) Naman and Slevin (1993) |
| | FLEX02 | 0.68*** | | | | |
| | FLEX03 | 0.74*** | | | | |
| | FLEX04 | 0.74*** | | | | |
| | FLEX05 | 0.56*** | | | | |
| | FLEX06 | (deleted) | | | | |
| | FLEX07 | 0.74*** | | | | |
| | FLEX08 | 0.74*** | | | | |
| | FLEX09 | 0.72*** | | | | |
| Entrepreneurial orientation (EO) | EO01 | 0.72*** | Cronbach's alpha = 0.854 rho_A = 0.908 | AVE = 0.52 C.R = 0.915 | Accepted | Naman and Slevin (1993); Khandwalla (1977);Miller (1983);Covin and Slevin (1988) |
| | EO02 | 0.64*** | | | | |
| | EO03 | 0.67*** | | | | |
| | EO04 | 0.66*** | | | | |
| | EO05 | 0.74*** | | | | |
| | EO06 | 0.79*** | | | | |
| | EO07 | 0.79*** | | | | |
| | EO08 | 0.71*** | | | | |
| | EO09 | 0.74*** | | | | |
| | EO10 | 0.77*** | | | | |
| Open innovation climate (Climate) | Climate01 | 0.85*** | Cronbach's alpha = 0.866 rho_A = 0.883 | AVE = 0.66 C.R = 0.905 | Accepted | Hung and Chiang (2010) |
| | Climate02 | 0.89*** | | | | |
| | Climate03 | 0.90*** | | | | |
| | Climate04 | (deleted) | | | | |
| | Climate05 | 0.79*** | | | | |
| | Climate06 | (deleted) | | | | |
| | Climate07 | 0.61*** | | | | |
| | Climate08 | (deleted) | | | | |

(1) ***p < 0.001.
(2) Details about discriminant validity (Fornell-Larcker and heterotrait-monotrait criteria) are shown in Table 4.
(3) Items with outer loadings <0.5 have been excluded from the analysis (such as FLEX06, Climate04, Climate06, and Climate08).

analysis, eight out of nine organisational flexibility items were significantly loaded on the construct with factor loadings larger than 0.56 (p-value < 0.001). EO will help firms overcome the possible risks and uncertainty involved in openness. When utilising external knowledge, firms cannot be free from risks, such as higher transaction costs, technology confidentiality, and various organisational cultures of external partners (Narula 2004; Oakey 2013). EO can be considered to represent a firm's tendency to take risks despite uncertainty embedded in the new innovation process and practice (Naman and Slevin 1993; Hung and Chiang 2010). EO consists of three sub-concepts – innovativeness, pro-activeness, and risk-taking propensity – which play an important role in establishing an aggressive and bold strategic direction (Covin and Slevin 1988; Naman and Slevin 1993). For the analysis, EO was measured using 10 items, which were originally devised by Khandwalla (1977) and employed in several previous studies (Miller 1983; Covin and Slevin 1988; Naman and Slevin 1993). Confirmatory factor analysis confirmed uni-dimensionality for EO.[1] All 10 items were loaded on one factor with loading values larger than 0.6 (p-value < 0.001). Table 1 shows the results of our measurement model. All constructs were deemed to be highly reliable and valid.

### *3.1.2. Open innovation activity*

To measure OI activity, the scale suggested by Laursen and Salter (2006) was adopted to construct the dependent variables: (1) external information search breadth (SearchB), (2) external information search depth (SearchD), (3) collaboration breadth (CollaboB), and (4) collaboration depth (CollaboD). Our measure of information search employed a survey question asking respondents about the use and importance of a variety of information sources for a firm's innovation activities. In total, 14 potential information sources were listed (see Appendix), and forms were designed to indicate the importance and frequency of use of each source on a 7-point Likert scale. First, to measure search breadth, each of the 14 sources was coded as a binary variable: '0' indicating no use, and '1' indicating use of the given knowledge source. Then, the 14 sources were simply added up, so that a firm obtained a '0' value when no knowledge sources were used, while it obtained the value of '14' when all the knowledge sources were used. Second, to measure information search depth, we gave each high response (importance value, 6–7) a value of '1', while all other responses were given a value of '0'. These scores were then added. Third, to measure collaboration breadth, each of the seven collaboration partners was coded as a binary variable: '0' indicating no use, and '1' indicating collaboration with the partner. Then, these seven partners were simply added up so that a firm obtained '0' when no knowledge sources were used, while it obtained '7' when all types of collaboration were used. Last, to measure collaboration depth, we gave each high response (importance value, 6–7) a value of '1', while all other responses were given a value of '0'. These scores were then added.

### *3.1.3. Moderators*

The facilitator variables – knowledge management process (KMP), knowledge management human resource (KMHR), and incentive – were measured using a 7-point Likert scale. Three

[1]In this study, EO was measured as having uni-dimensionality for model parsimony. There were no differences between the analyses of the cases of EO comprising three dimensions (second-order confirmatory factor analysis) and one dimension (first-order confirmatory factor analysis).

items were employed to evaluate formal appropriability – copyright/trademarks, patents, and utility model right – and four items for informal appropriability – non-disclosure agreement, secrecy, complexity of design, and lead-time advantages over competitors. Each item was measured on a 7-point Likert scale to determine how it was utilised to protect innovation over the past three years. Then, mean value of formal and informal appropriability was used in the measurements. All the measurements are illustrated in Appendix.

### 3.4. Sampling and data collection procedures

To build a more reliable data set, we used multiple data sources: lists of 'inno-biz' and 'R&D-oriented' firms. Inno-biz firms represent technology-intensive and innovation-oriented SMEs, which are accredited by the Korean government agency, Ministry of SMEs and Start-ups (MSS), based on the innovativeness evaluation criteria of the Organisation for Economic Cooperation and Development (OECD). A total of 1,400 firms were randomly selected from the inno-biz firm database published by the MSS. Further, another 4,600 firms were randomly selected from the database of 'R&D-oriented firms' (i.e. firms that established their own R&D divisions) published by the Korea Industrial Technology Association. Through such sampling procedures, a total of 6,000 structured questionnaires were mailed to potential respondents using an online survey system. The initial response rate was 13.9%, and comparing early and late responses indicated no serious statistical difference, suggesting that there is no serious non-response bias (Armstrong and Overton 1977). As utilisation of external knowledge requires certain level of absorptive capacity, this study focused on innovative manufacturing SMEs with high R&D intensity. Therefore, data cleaning was performed by eliminating large and service firms. Survey responses below 40% for the main question were also removed. After data cleaning, 389 responses were used for the analysis. Sample characteristics are listed in Tables 2 and 3.

### 3.5. Analysis method

PLS-SEM was employed for analysing the data. Unlike covariance-based structural equation modelling (CB-SEM), PLS-SEM does not presume that the data are

**Table 2.** Sample characteristics (n = 389).

| Descriptive statistics | | | | Technology level[4] | | |
|---|---|---|---|---|---|---|
| Variable | Obs. | Mean | Std. Dev. | Level | Freq. | % |
| Firm Age | 389 | 14.98 | 8.90 | High Tech. | 99 | 25.45 |
| Capital[1] | 387 | 1958.89 | 5,681.03 | Medium High Tech. | 107 | 27.51 |
| Sales[2] | 389 | 11,406.83 | 24,425.67 | Medium Low Tech. | 115 | 29.56 |
| No. of Employees | 389 | 35.80 | 45.67 | Low Tech. | 42 | 10.80 |
| R&D Intensity[3] | 351 | 20.49 | 17.64 | No response | 26 | 6.68 |

1) and 2) unit: \$1,000; 3) R&D intensity = $\frac{\text{R\&D employees}}{\textit{Total employees}} \times 100$

4) The four technology levels – low, low-mid, mid-high and high – were grouped based on OECD classification.

**Table 3.** Profile of the sample of respondent companies.

| Industry | Freq. | Percent |
|---|---|---|
| Food, drink, and tobacco | 17 | 4.37 |
| Wood, textiles, and furniture | 7 | 1.80 |
| Electricity, gas, water supply, and environmental purification | 9 | 2.31 |
| Paper and printing | 15 | 3.86 |
| Refined petroleum products | 11 | 2.83 |
| Chemicals | 20 | 5.14 |
| Leather, fur products, and clothing apparel | 19 | 4.88 |
| Non-metallic minerals | 11 | 2.83 |
| Basic metal | 12 | 3.08 |
| Fabric, metal products, and plastics | 39 | 10.03 |
| Machinery | 23 | 5.91 |
| Electrical | 60 | 15.42 |
| Motor vehicles, trailers, and other transport | 13 | 3.34 |
| Medical, pharmaceuticals, and medical precision and optical | 5 | 1.29 |
| Systems integration, information technology, and computer programming | 34 | 8.74 |
| Repair and reproduction | 13 | 3.34 |
| Other | 55 | 14.14 |
| Non-response | 26 | 6.68 |
| Total | 389 | 100 |

normally distributed. One key conjecture of this study is that more moderators would be necessary as the intensity/degree of openness increases. We believe that this integrative approach has not been adopted in many studies, and this complex research model can be better explored by the flexible and explorative PLS method. PLS-SEM provides four approaches to identify the interaction effects. Based on comparison of the four different approaches[2] of PLS-based interaction effects using Monte Carlo simulation, Henseler and Chin (2010) showed that the orthogonalising approach produces more accurate estimates while minimising the potential collinearity problem. Thus, this study employs the orthogonalising approach and utilises an additional two-stage approach for a robustness check. In addition, we pay attention to the fact that PLS can provide useful information, such as for IPMA. IPMA provides information about the relative importance of different constructs of the research model (Ringle and Sarstedt 2016), which enables us to expand our interpretation.

## 4. Results

### 4.1. Measurement model

The measurement results are reported in Table 1. The latent variables – FLEX, EO, and Climate – have good convergent validity, and internal consistency reliability. For all latent variables, Cronbach's alphas, rho_A, and composite reliabilities (C.R) are above 0.8, exceeding the suggested cut-off value of 0.7. Most outer loadings are

[2]These include the product indicator, two-stage, hybrid, and orthogonalising approaches.

satisfactory (i.e. over 0.60), and average variances extracted (AVE) values are higher than 0.5, which indicates that the construct explains more than half of the variance of its indicators (Latan, Ringle, and Jabbour 2016; Hair et al. 2017). According to the Fornell-Larcker criterion, the square root of each construct's AVE should be greater than its highest correlation with any other construct. As shown in Table 4, the square roots of AVEs are greater than the correlations between constructs, indicating that all constructs share more variance with their own measures than with others (Fornell and Larcker 1981). For a robustness check, a further discriminant validity check is conducted using the heterotrait-monotrait ratio of correlations (HTMT). Henseler, Ringle, and Sarstedt (2015) argued that traditional approaches, such as the Fornell-Larcker criterion, may not properly detect the lack of discriminant validity and showed that HTMT can be a better alternative in PLS-SEM. Our results show that the model has good discriminant validity (HTMT values < 0.85).

### 4.2. Structural model

Assessment results for the structural model are given in Table 5. R-squared and adjusted R-squared values for dependent variables are satisfactory, and Q predictive validity is also considered satisfactory. The variance inflation factor (VIF) values generated for all predictors are lower than 3.3, indicating that there is no serious collinearity issue among the independent variables. On the suggestions of Hu and Bentler (1999) and Henseler et al. (2014), the SRMR and rms Theta (as a measure of absolute fit) and NFI (Bentler and Bonett 1980) – as a measure of incremental fit – were used as a criteria to determine the goodness of fit of the structural model in PLS-SEM. Additionally the unweighted least squares discrepancy d_ULS and the geodesic discrepancy d_G should be included in the 95% bootstrap quantile (Henseler, Hubona, and Ray 2017). For example, d_ULS of 'SearchB' is 1.738 which is smaller than 1.964 - 95% bootstrap quantile (HI95). Table 5 shows the fit of the structural model, and the results suggest that, in overall aspect, the current structural model satisfies the condition of good model fit.

### 4.3. Analysis result

Results of the structural model analysis are shown in Figure 2. The analysis is conducted using a bootstrapping approach for 5,000 subsamples at the significance level of 5% two-tails. In Figure 2, (a)–(e) indicate the path coefficients of the model. Paths (a), (b), and (e) are positive and significant, which shows that organisational characteristics, such as OI-friendly climate, organisational flexibility and EO positively affect OI activities.

The moderating effects on the relationship between OI climate and activities are estimated. This study employs the orthogonalising approach and utilises an additional two-stage approach for a robustness check. As shown in Table 6, estimates from the two different methods are not significantly different in terms of size, statistical significance, and associational direction.

The analysis results support our conjecture that higher the openness intensity, the more organisational facilitators moderate the relationship between OI climate

**Table 4.** Correlation and discriminant validity results (N = 389).

| Variables | Mean | Std.D | Min | Max | 1 | 2 | 3 | 4 | 5 | 6 | 7 | 8 | 9 | 10 | 11 |
|---|---|---|---|---|---|---|---|---|---|---|---|---|---|---|---|
| 1. FLEX | 4.09 | 1.19 | 1 | 7 | **(0.705)** | ***0.704*** | ***0.355*** | | | | | | | | |
| 2. EO | 4.32 | 1.17 | 1 | 7 | 0.6201** | **(0.726)** | ***0.350*** | | | | | | | | |
| 3. Climate | 5.21 | 1.06 | 1.2 | 7 | 0.3029** | 0.3109** | **(0.813)** | | | | | | | | |
| 4. SearchB | 6.75 | 4.27 | 0 | 14 | 0.1639** | 0.2490** | 0.1867** | - | | | | | | | |
| 5. SearchD | 3.19 | 3.26 | 0 | 14 | 0.2340** | 0.3145** | 0.3376** | 0.4072** | - | | | | | | |
| 6. CollaboB | 3.01 | 2.11 | 0 | 7 | 0.1420** | 0.2194** | 0.1868** | 0.7186** | 0.3655** | - | | | | | |
| 7. CollaboD | 1.17 | 1.55 | 0 | 7 | 0.2629** | 0.3178** | 0.3408** | 0.3388** | 0.5721** | 0.3802** | - | | | | |
| 8. Incentive | 3.75 | 1.72 | 1 | 7 | 0.5017** | 0.5176** | 0.1921** | 0.1125 | 0.2350** | 0.1155 | 0.2712** | - | | | |
| 9. KMP | 3.66 | 1.54 | 1 | 7 | 0.3556** | 0.4938** | 0.3033** | 0.2077** | 0.2568** | 0.1963** | 0.2882** | 0.4410** | - | | |
| 10. KMHR | 3.66 | 1.68 | 1 | 7 | 0.2098** | 0.4076** | 0.2533** | 0.2166** | 0.2454** | 0.1709** | 0.2490** | 0.3287** | 0.7403** | - | |
| 11. FORAPP | 3.50 | 1.75 | 1 | 7 | 0.0635 | 0.2139** | 0.0451 | 0.1600** | 0.1706** | 0.1943** | 0.1899** | 0.1335 | 0.2405** | 0.1929** | - |
| 12. INFORAPP | 3.45 | 1.47 | 1 | 7 | 0.1773** | 0.3811** | 0.1717** | 0.2028** | 0.2492** | 0.2086** | 0.2619** | 0.2831** | 0.3520** | 0.2753** | 0.3218** |

(1) Pairwise correlations: ** indicates significance at the 0.01% level (two tailed).
(2) Square roots of average variances extracted are shown in parenthesis on the shaded diagonal.
(3) The bold and italic numbers indicate heterotrait-monotrait criterion values.

**Table 5.** Structural model results.

| Variables | $R^2$ | Adj. $R^2$ | Effect size ($f^2$) | | $Q^2$ | VIF (<3.3) | AFVIF (<3.3) | SRMR (<0.08) | NFI (~0.9) | rms Theta (<0.12) | d_ULS (Value < HI95) | | d_G (Value < HI95) | |
|---|---|---|---|---|---|---|---|---|---|---|---|---|---|---|
| | | | OIA | OIC | | | | | | | Value | HI95 | Value | HI95 |
| FLEX | - | - | 0.003 | 0.026 | - | 1.695 | - | - | - | - | - | - | - | - |
| EO | - | - | 0.032 | 0.029 | - | 1.702 | - | - | - | - | - | - | - | - |
| Climate | 0.125 | 0.120 | 0.072 | - | 0.074 | 1.143 | - | - | - | - | - | - | - | - |
| SearchB | 0.075 | 0.068 | - | - | 0.059 | - | 2.022 | 0.064 | 0.805 | 0.113 | 1.738 | 1.964 | 0.658 | 0.664 |
| SearchD | 0.162 | 0.156 | - | - | 0.144 | - | 2.022 | 0.064 | 0.807 | 0.114 | 1.59 | 1.839 | 0.64 | 0.645 |
| CollaboB | 0.065 | 0.058 | - | - | 0.046 | - | 2.022 | 0.063 | 0.805 | 0.114 | 1.947 | 2.116 | 0.697 | 0.702 |
| CollaboD | 0.170 | 0.164 | - | - | 0.154 | | 2.022 | 0.064 | 0.806 | 0.119 | 1.774 | 1.775 | 0.645 | 0.661 |

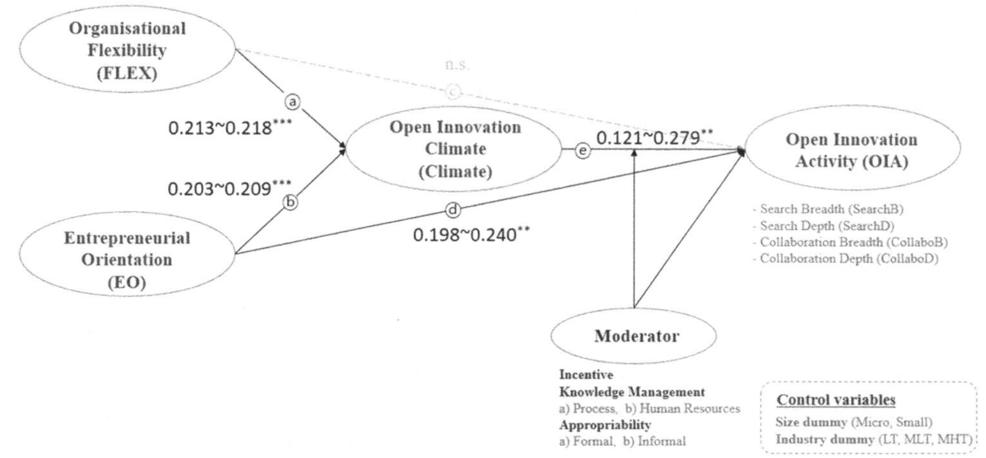


**Figure 2.** PLS-SEM path analysis results.

**Table 6.** Moderation effect results.

| | Open innovation activities<br>An increase of intensity of openness → | | | | |
|---|---|---|---|---|---|
| Moderator variables | SearchB | SearchD | CollaboB | CollaboD | Hypothesis testing |
| KMP | 0.130** | 0.129*** | 0.134*** | 0.183*** | Supported |
| | (0.124**) | (0.141**) | (0.135***) | (0.188***) | |
| KMHR | 0.118** | 0.113** | 0.164*** | 0.194*** | |
| | (0.120**) | (0.123**) | (0.158***) | (0.195***) | |
| Incentive | 0.074 | 0.092* | 0.102** | 0.123*** | |
| | (0.050) | (0.095*) | (0.095**) | (0.124***) | |
| INFORAPP | 0.095 | 0.101 | 0.096** | 0.146*** | |
| | (0.094) | (0.078) | (0.105**) | (0.146***) | |
| FORAPP | 0.075 | 0.087 | 0.077 | 0.151*** | |
| | (0.074) | (0.016) | (0.015) | (0.149***) | |

(1) Significance level: *p < 0.1, **<0.05, and ***p < 0.01.
(2) Shadowed cells indicate statistically significant moderating effects.
(3) All estimates are standardised beta coefficients, and values in parentheses are two-stage approach results.
(4) Each moderator's direct path is included in the analysis.

and OI activities. Both knowledge management variables (KMP and KMHR) are statistically significant and positively associated with all OI activities. The moderating effect of incentive on the relationship between OI climate and OI activity (i.e. Climate → OIA) is between 0.092 and 0.123 and is statistically significant for search depth and collaboration breadth/depth. The moderating effect of the appropriability strategy is not observed for external information search, both in breadth and depth, but it shows statistical significance for collaboration. Accordingly, the results in Table 6 show 'stair shape' pattern of organisational facilitators. The number of statistically significant facilitators (i.e. shaded cells in Table 6) increases as the intensity of OI activity increases. Only two variables, KMP and KMHR, are significant moderators for OI of the lowest intensity, search breadth. For the highest intensity OI, collaboration depth, all five examined facilitators are significant moderators.

### 4.4. Further analysis

Several additional analyses were performed. First, IPMA is conducted. IPMA compares the importance and performance of construct variables (Ringle and Sarstedt 2016), and it enables us to understand what is important. In Figure 3, the target construct involves four different OI activities, and IPMA shows the relative importance and performance of FLEX, EO, and Climate for the target; horizontal-axis indicates 'importance' and vertical-axis, 'performance'. Clear pattern differences between breadth and depth are observed. The results show that the importance of some constructs varies according to the type of OI activity. EO shows high importance in both breadth and depth, but the importance of FLEX and Climate is smaller in breadth than in depth. Depth activities require high level of EO and Climate and intermediate level of flexibility, which suggests that search and collaboration depth require more active organisational propensity than broad OI activities.

Second, PLS multi-group analysis is conducted to determine whether there are any differences according to industry type or firm size. Our research model (Figure 2) already includes dummy control variables, but, for a robustness check, PLS multi-group analysis – the most conservative non-parametric analysis comparing group differences based on bootstrapping (Sarstedt, Henseler, and Ringle 2011) – was additionally conducted. Coefficient differences based on different firm sizes and industry type groups are compared using 5,000 bootstrapped sub-samples, and the results indicate that there are almost no differences between the groups in terms of statistical significance (see Table 7).

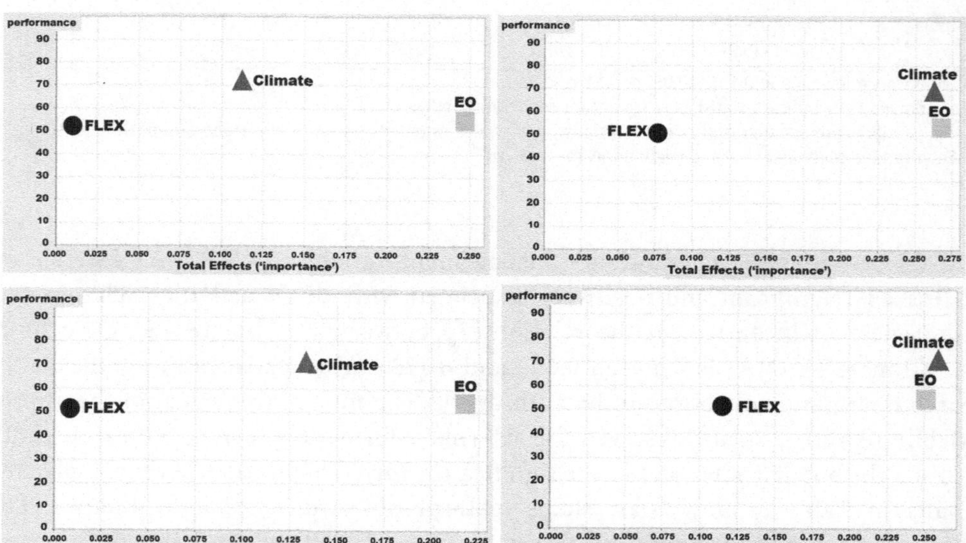


Figure 3. Results of the importance-performance map analysis (IPMA).

**Table 7.** PLS-MGA results.

| Dependent variable (OI activity) | Moderators | Coefficient differences between industry groups -High-tech industry: 206 -Low-tech industry: 157 | Coefficient differences and firm-size difference -SMEs (emp>10): 276 -Micro (emp≤10): 113 |
|---|---|---|---|
| SearchB | KMP | 0.100 | 0.024 |
| | KMHR | 0.039 | 0.126 |
| | Incentive | 0.034 | 0.073 |
| | INFORAPP | 0.021 | 0.009 |
| | FORAPP | 0.045 | 0.221 |
| SearchD | KMP | 0.062 | 0.075 |
| | KMHR | 0.029 | 0.106 |
| | Incentive | 0.039 | 0.073 |
| | INFORAPP | 0.030 | 0.319** |
| | FORAPP | 0.033 | 0.294 |
| CollaboB | KMP | 0.032 | 0.026 |
| | KMHR | 0.049 | 0.036 |
| | Incentive | 0.027 | 0.021 |
| | INFORAPP | 0.072 | 0.044 |
| | FORAPP | 0.219 | 0.085 |
| CollaboD | KMP | 0.113 | 0.030 |
| | KMHR | 0.084 | 0.043 |
| | Incentive | 0.136 | 0.089 |
| | INFORAPP | 0.072 | 0.055 |
| | FORAPP | 0.096 | 0.104 |

Statistical significance: * $p < 0.1$, ** $p < 0.05$, and *** $p < 0.01$.

Last, regression analysis is conducted for another robustness check. Table 8 shows the effect of moderator variables on different open innovation activities. Regression analysis showed the same moderator patterns (i.e. 'stair shape') in terms of statistical significance and correlation direction (i.e. ±). Of course, there are small differences in terms of coefficient values because of the difference in model structure, but there is almost no difference of moderation effects in terms of statistical significance and correlation direction between the PLS-SEM and regression analysis results.

## 5. Conclusions

### *5.1. Discussion and implications*

Recently, many studies have explored OI application in SMEs and showed that OI can be a good strategic option for their innovation (e.g., Parida, Westerberg, and Frishammar 2012; Ahn, Minshall, and Mortara 2015). However, while much attention has been paid to whether OI enhances performance (e.g., Mazzola, Bruccoleri, and Perrone 2012), the internal mechanism of OI has not yet been fully investigated (West and Bogers 2017). Despite its popularity, the OI process still sees a more trial-and-error approach compared with a well-managed traditional innovation process (Gassmann, Enkel, and Chesbrough 2010). To address this research gap, the current study attempts to explore OI implementation in SMEs by investigating the changing moderating effects

**Table 8.** Regression results.

| | SearchB | | | | | SearchD | | | | | CollaboB | | | | | CollaboD | | | | |
|---|---|---|---|---|---|---|---|---|---|---|---|---|---|---|---|---|---|---|---|---|
| | Model 1 | Model 2 | Model 3 | Model 4 | Model 5 | Model 6 | Model 7 | Model 8 | Model 9 | Model 10 | Model 11 | Model 12 | Model 13 | Model 14 | Model 15 | Model 16 | Model 17 | Model 18 | Model 19 | Model 20 |
| Climate | 0.679*** | 0.681*** | 0.702*** | 0.806*** | 0.853*** | 0.992*** | 0.995*** | 0.966*** | 0.976*** | 1.102*** | 0.346*** | 0.377*** | 0.354*** | 0.405*** | 0.399*** | 0.484*** | 0.505*** | 0.456*** | 0.509*** | 0.505*** |
| KMP | 0.395*** | | | | | 0.303*** | | | | | 0.177*** | | | | | 0.167*** | | | | |
| KMHR | | 0.406*** | | | | | 0.289*** | | | | | 0.133** | | | | | 0.128*** | | | |
| Incentive | | | 0.176 | | | | | 0.308*** | | | | | 0.0838 | | | | | 0.174*** | | |
| INFORAPP | | | | 0.496*** | | | | | 0.426*** | | | | | 0.252*** | | | | | 0.217*** | |
| FORAPP | | | | | 0.362*** | | | | | 0.275*** | | | | | 0.224*** | | | | | 0.149*** |
| KMP xClimate | **0.264*** | | | | | **0.227**** | | | | | **0.136**** | | | | | **0.152***** | | | | |
| KMHR xClimate | | **0.239**** | | | | | **0.189**** | | | | | **0.151***** | | | | | **0.146***** | | | |
| Incentive xClimate | | | 0.138 | | | | | **0.171**** | | | | | **0.114**** | | | | | **0.111***** | | |
| INFORAPP xClimate | | | | 0.219 | | | | | 0.116 | | | | | **0.128**** | | | | | **0.132***** | |
| FORAPP xClimate | | | | | 0.163 | | | | | 0.0368 | | | | | 0.0135 | | | | | **0.134***** |
| Constant | 3.082*** | 3.091*** | 3.013*** | 2.600** | 2.343** | −2.091* | −2.083** | −1.899** | −1.963 | −2.64*** | 1.136** | 0.976* | 1.111** | 0.942* | 0.976* | −1.43*** | −1.53*** | −1.25*** | −1.50*** | −1.45*** |
| Observations | 389 | 389 | 387 | 359 | 359 | 389 | 389 | 387 | 359 | 359 | 389 | 389 | 387 | 359 | 359 | 389 | 389 | 387 | 359 | 359 |
| R-squared | 0.07 | 0.076 | 0.044 | 0.077 | 0.072 | 0.153 | 0.152 | 0.156 | 0.154 | 0.161 | 0.067 | 0.068 | 0.053 | 0.081 | 0.076 | 0.178 | 0.174 | 0.181 | 0.175 | 0.169 |

(1) Robust standard errors (* $p < 0.1$, ** $p < 0.05$, *** $p < 0.01$).
(2) Unstandardized beta.

of organisational facilitators in innovative SMEs. OI implementation can be perceived as an attempt to change the innovation routine. Therefore, our focus is given to the role of moderators that accelerate/facilitate a high level of openness.

First, the 'stair-shape' moderation effects (see Table 6) suggest that the organisational efforts firms must put in are proportional to the level of openness intensity. Knowledge management plays a baseline moderator role, and its moderation effects are significant throughout all OI activities. However, if firms aim to implement a higher level of openness, more systematic organisational efforts are necessary. For example, in terms of collaboration, a light touch, such as lead time or complexity of design, would be enough moderator for firms to initiate collaboration with multiple partners. However, when firms aim to achieve strong engagement with specific partners, a formalised knowledge appropriation strategy will positively moderate the relationship between a firm's OI proclivity and a high level of openness, such as repetitive collaboration. This suggests that there is room for optimisation for openness. Despite many successful OI stories, not all firms become successful in OI implementation, and our results show that there is an optimal fit between organisational efforts and the intensity of openness in OI activities. For example, organising a patent management team or employee training for IP management would be beneficial for openness. However, these investments would be more effectively working when firms aim at strong collaboration engagement. Therefore, firms, particularly SMEs that may lack resources needed to engage in OI successfully, must first decide what OI activity they will conduct and then invest in the necessary organisational configuration to achieve resource optimisation. Because it is not easy for SMEs to employ multiple organisational practices simultaneously (Rothwell and Dodgson 1995), it would be better for them to have a gentle start with a low level of openness (e.g. broad external search) and then gradually increase the degree of openness by proportionally increasing resource investment.

Second, our results identified the importance of knowledge management in OI process. As shown in Table 6, the moderation effects of knowledge management (both for process and human resources) are significant in all the examined OI activities. The moderation effect of other factors, such as formal appropriation, is statistically significant only in a highly intensive OI activity. This finding suggests that firms with effective knowledge management can easily increase the intensity of OI activities, but those that neglect this basic element may not easily to pivot their OI activity or might take longer for their transformation for OI. By its definition, OI stresses knowledge flow via a permeable boundary (Chesbrough, Vanhaverbeke, and West 2006), so systematic management of knowledge can be important for OI. This finding is particularly influential for SMEs, in the sense that they lack resources for organisational changes (Lee et al. 2010). Large firms may be able to employ multiple innovation routes for better performance, but SMEs cannot typically take this approach (Minshall et al. 2010). Thus, they must optimise their innovation, and in this context, managing knowledge would be an essential organisational configuration. Because knowledge management plays a fundamental moderator role in OI, SMEs must invest in this organisational configuration to initiate OI and to easily pivot to a highly intensive OI activity later.

Last, IPMA results suggest that organisational factors show their variable importance according to the intensity of OI activities. Broad search indicates superficial knowledge exploration, while deep search indicates repetitive access to particular external information sources (Cruz-González et al. 2015). Unlike search, collaboration demands stronger mutual interactions, continuous communication, and a trust-building process (Ahn, Minshall, and Mortara 2018). In this respect, we suggest different openness intensities (see Figure 1), and our IPMA results are in line with that assumption. As shown in Figure 3, the importance of OI climate increases as the openness intensity increases. Its importance (i.e. total effects along the horizontal axis) for highly intensive OI was higher than those for less intensive OI (e.g. 0.120 in search breadth vs. 0.260 in search depth and 0.265 in collaboration depth), which indicates that a higher level of OI activity demands more intense OI climate. Also, in the IPMA results, EO shows an average level performance of around 50, but its importance is high in all OI activities. Therefore, a one-unit increase in the performance of EO would result in a high increase in the OI activity performance. This finding suggests important practical implications for CEOs and managers of SMEs. If they would like to enhance the performance of OI activity, their top priority must be improving the performance captured by EO. It is because this organisational factor has the highest importance but a relatively low (around average) performance (Ringle and Sarstedt 2016).

### *5.2. Research limitations*

Despite the findings and implications, we cannot deny that this study suffers from some research limitations. First, this study does not examine the full spectrum of OI activities. External information search (in-bound) and collaboration (coupled process) are explored in this research, but out-bound OI, such as licensing-out or open sourcing, is not investigated. Second, the link to OI performance was not explored. This study was motivated by the fact that the majority research attempts to explore the output of OI rather than its process. In this vein, the current research focused on the inside of OI mechanism, but future study exploring the whole process of OI from initiation to output would offer more in-depth understanding of OI implementation. Third, due to limitations of research resources, cross-sectional data are analysed in this study. Since the longitudinal or dynamic mechanism is not explored, endogeneity can cause a reverse causality problem. Admittedly, one of the effective ways of addressing this issue would be using panel datasets. If researchers can use OI activity data with time lags, better results minimising potential endogeneity may be obtained. Finally, the current study focuses on manufacturing SMEs; thus, whether the findings from this study can be expanded to other types of firms, such as large firms or service firms, is not examined. It is necessary to investigate how much hypothesis of this study describes the large or service firms. Future research addressing these issues can present detailed findings and provide a deeper understanding of the OI mechanism.

## Disclosure statement

No potential conflict of interest was reported by the authors.

## Funding

This research was funded by Nation Research Foundation in Korea (NRF-2017R1C1B5018009).

## ORCID

Joon Mo Ahn http://orcid.org/0000-0003-4154-3995

## References

Ahn, J. M., L. Mortara, and T. Minshall. 2018. "Dynamic Capabilities and Economic Crises: Has Openness Enhanced a Firm's Performance in an Economic Downturn?" *Industrial and Corporate Change* 27: 49–63. doi: 10.1093/icc/dtx048.

Ahn, J. M., N. Roijakkers, R. Fini, and L. Mortara. 2019. "Leveraging Open Innovation to Improve Society: Past Achievements and Future Trajectories." *R&D Management* 49: 267–278. doi:10.1111/radm.12373.

Ahn, J. M., T. Minshall, and L. Mortara. 2015. "Open Innovation: A New Classification and Its Impact on Firm Performance in Innovative Smes." *Journal of Innovation Management* 3: 33–54. doi:10.24840/2183-0606_003.002.

Ahn, J. M., Y. Ju, T. H. Moon, T. Minshall, D. Probert, S. Y. Sohn, and L. Mortara. 2016. "Beyond Absorptive Capacity in Open Innovation Process: The Relationships between Openness, Capacities and Firm Performance." *Technology Analysis & Strategic Management* 28: 1009–1028. doi:10.1080/09537325.2016.1181737.

Armstrong, J. S., and T. S. Overton. 1977. "Estimating Nonresponse Bias in Mail Surveys." *Journal of Marketing Research* 14: 396–402. doi:10.1177/002224377701400320.

Barney, J. 1991. "Firm Resources and Sustained Competitive Advantage." *Journal of Management* 17: 99–120. doi:10.1177/014920639101700108.

Bentler, P. M., and D. G. Bonett. 1980. "Significance Tests and Goodness of Fit in the Analysis of Covariance Structures." *Psychological Bulletin* 88: 588–606. doi:10.1037/0033-2909.88.3.588.

Bianchi, M., D. Chiaroni, V. Chiesa, and F. Frattini. 2011. "Exploring the Role of Human Resources in Technology out-Licensing: An Empirical Analysis of Biotech Newtechnology-Based Firms." *Technology Analysis & Strategic Management* 23: 825–849. doi:10.1080/09537325.2011.604153.

Bogers, M., A.-K. Zobel, A. Afuah, E. Almirall, S. Brunswicker, L. Dahlander, L. Frederiksen, et al. 2017. "The Open Innovation Research Landscape: Established Perspectives and Emerging Themes across Different Levels of Analysis". *Industry and Innovation* 24: 8–40. doi:10.1080/13662716.2016.1240068.

Chesbrough, H. 2003. *Open Innovation: The New Imperative for Creating and Profiting from Technology*. Boston, Mass: Harvard Business School Press.

Chesbrough, H., W. Vanhaverbeke, and J. West. 2006. *Open Innovation: Researching a New Paradigm*. Oxford: Oxford University Press.

Chiaroni, D., V. Chiesa, and F. Frattini. 2011. "The Open Innovation Journey: How Firms Dynamically Implement the Emerging Innovation Management Paradigm." *Technovation* 31: 34–43. doi:10.1016/j.technovation.2009.08.007.

Cohen, W. M., and D. A. Levinthal. 1990. "Absorptive Capacity: A New Perspective on Learning and Innovation." *Administrative Science Quarterly* 35: 128–152. doi:10.2307/2393553.

Covin, J. G., and D. P. Slevin. 1988. "The Influence of Organization Structure on the Utility of an Entrepreneurial Top Management Style." *Journal of Management Studies* 25: 217–234. doi:10.1111/joms.1988.25.issue-3.

Cruz-González, J., P. López-Sáez, J. E. Navas-López, and M. Delgado-Verde. 2015. "Open Search Strategies and Firm Performance: The Different Moderating Role of Technological Environmental Dynamism." *Technovation* 35: 32–45. doi:10.1016/j.technovation.2014.09.001.

Dahlander, L., and D. M. Gann. 2010. "How Open Is Innovation?" *Research Policy* 39: 699–709. doi:10.1016/j.respol.2010.01.013.

Damanpour, F. 1991. "Organizational Innovation: A Meta-Analysis of Effects of Determinants and Moderators." *Academy of Management Journal* 34: 555–590.

Deichmann, D., I. Rozentale, and R. Barnhoorn. 2017. "Open Innovation Generates Great Ideas, So Why Aren't Companies Adopting Them?" *Harvard Business Review*. [Online] https://hbr.org/2017/12/open-innovation-generates-great-ideas-so-why-arent-companies-adopting-them.

Di Minin, A., F. Frattini, and A. Piccaluga. 2010. "Fiat: Open Innovation in a Downturn (1993–2003)." *California Management Review* 52: 132–159. doi:10.1525/cmr.2010.52.3.132.

Felin, T., and T. R. Zenger. 2014. "Closed or Open Innovation? Problem Solving and the Governance Choice." *Research Policy* 43: 914–925. doi:10.1016/j.respol.2013.09.006.

Fishbein, M., and I. Ajzen. 1975. *Belief, Attitude, Intention, and Behavior: An Introduction to Theory and Research*. Boston, Mass: Addison-Wesley Pub.

Fornell, C., and D. F. Larcker. 1981. "Evaluating Structural Equation Models with Unobservable Variables and Measurement Error." *Journal of Marketing Research* 18: 39–50. doi:10.1177/002224378101800104.

Foss, N. J., K. Laursen, and T. Pedersen. 2011. "Linking Customer Interaction and Innovation: The Mediating Role of New Organizational Practices." *Organization Science* 22: 980–999. doi:10.1287/orsc.1100.0584.

Fu, X. 2012. "How Does Openness Affect the Importance of Incentives for Innovation?" *Research Policy* 41: 512–523. doi:10.1016/j.respol.2011.12.011.

Galende, J., and J. M. De La Fuente. 2003. "Internal Factors Determining a Firm's Innovative Behaviour." *Research Policy* 32: 715–736. doi:10.1016/S0048-7333(02)00082-3.

Gassmann, O., E. Enkel, and H. Chesbrough. 2010. "The Future of Open Innovation." *R&D Management* 40: 213–221. doi:10.1111/j.1467-9310.2010.00605.x.

Hair, J. F., C. L. Hollingsworth, A. B. Randolph, and A. Y. L. Chong. 2017. "An Updated and Expanded Assessment of Pls-Sem in Information Systems Research." *Industrial Management & Data Systems* 117: 442–458. doi:10.1108/IMDS-04-2016-0130.

Henseler, J., C. M. Ringle, and M. Sarstedt. 2015. "A New Criterion for Assessing Discriminant Validity in Variance-Based Structural Equation Modeling." *Journal of the Academy of Marketing Science* 43: 115–135. doi:10.1007/s11747-014-0403-8.

Henseler, J., G. Hubona, and P. A. Ray. 2017. "Partial Least Squares Path Modeling: Updated Guidelines." In *PartialLeast Squares Path Modeling*, edited by H. Latan and R. Noonan, 19–39. Berlin: Springer.

Henseler, J., T. K. Dijkstra, M. Sarstedt, C. M. Ringle, A. Diamantopoulos, D. W. Straub, D. J. Ketchen, et al. 2014. "Common Beliefs and Reality about Pls: Commentson Rönkkö and Evermann (2013)". *Organizational Research Methods* 17: 182–209. doi:10.1177/1094428114526928.

Henseler, J., and W. W. Chin. 2010. "A Comparison of Approaches for the Analysis of Interaction Effects between Latent Variables Using Partial Least Squares Path Modeling." *Structural Equation Modeling: A Multidisciplinary Journal* 17: 82–109. doi:10.1080/10705510903439003.

Holgersson, M., O. Granstrand, and M. Bogers. 2018. "The Evolution of Intellectual Property Strategy in Innovation Ecosystems: Uncovering Complementary and Substitute Appropriability Regimes." *Long Range Planning* 51: 303–319. doi:10.1016/j.lrp.2017.08.007.

Hu, L. T., and P. M. Bentler. 1999. "Cutoff Criteria for Fit Indexes in Covariance Structure Analysis: Conventional Criteria versus New Alternatives." *Structural Equation Modeling: a Multidisciplinary Journal* 6: 1–55. doi:10.1080/10705519909540118.

Huizingh, E. K. 2011. "Open Innovation: State of the Art and Future Perspectives." *Technovation* 31: 2–9. doi:10.1016/j.technovation.2010.10.002.

Hung, K.-P., and Y.-H. Chiang. 2010. "Open Innovation Proclivity, Entrepreneurial Orientation, and Perceived Firm Performance." *International Journal of Technology Management* 52: 257–274. doi:10.1504/IJTM.2010.035976.

Kang, K. N., and H. Park. 2012. "Influence of Government R&D Support and Inter-Firm Collaborations on Innovation in Korean Biotechnology Smes." *Technovation* 32: 68–78. doi:10.1016/j.technovation.2011.08.004.

Khandwalla, P. N. 1977. *The Design of Organizations*. Boston: Houghton Mifflin Harcourt Publishing Company.

Kratzer, J., D. Meissner, and V. Roud. 2017. "Open Innovation and Company Culture: Internal Openness Makes the Difference." *Technological Forecasting and Social Change* 119: 128–138. doi:10.1016/j.techfore.2017.03.022.

Latan, H., C. M. Ringle, and C. J. C. Jabbour. 2016. "Whistleblowing Intentions among Public Accountants in Indonesia: Testing for the Moderation Effects." *Journal of Business Ethics* 134: 1–16.

Laursen, K., and A. Salter. 2006. "Open for Innovation: The Role of Openness in Explaining Innovation Performance among Uk Manufacturing Firms." *Strategic Management Journal* 27: 131–150. doi:10.1002/(ISSN)1097-0266.

Laursen, K., and A. J. Salter. 2014. "The Paradox of Openness: Appropriability, External Search and Collaboration." *Research Policy* 43: 867–878. doi:10.1016/j.respol.2013.10.004.

Laursen, K., and N. J. Foss. 2003. "New Human Resource Management Practices, Complementarities and the Impact on Innovation Performance." *Cambridge Journal of Economics* 27: 243–263. doi:10.1093/cje/27.2.243.

Lee, S., G. Park, B. Yoon, and J. Park. 2010. "Open Innovation in Smes – An Intermediated Network Model." *Research Policy* 39: 290–300. doi:10.1016/j.respol.2009.12.009.

Martini, A., P. Neirotti, and F. P. Appio. 2017. "Knowledge Searching, Integrating and Performing: Always a Tuned Trio for Innovation?" *Long Range Planning* 50: 200–220. doi:10.1016/j.lrp.2015.12.020.

Mazzola, E., M. Bruccoleri, and G. Perrone. 2012. "The Effect of Inbound, Outbound and Coupled Innovation on Performance." *International Journal of Innovation Management* 16: 1–27. doi:10.1142/S1363919612400087.

Miller, D. 1983. "The Correlates of Entrepreneurship in Three Types of Firms." *Management Science* 29: 770–791. doi:10.1287/mnsc.29.7.770.

Minshall, T., L. Mortara, R. Valli, and D. Probert. 2010. "Making "Asymmetric" Partnerships Work." *Research-Technology Management* 53: 53–63. doi:10.1080/08956308.2010.11657631.

Mowery, D. C., J. E. Oxley, and B. S. Silverman. 1998. "Technological Overlap and Interfirm Cooperation: Implications for the Resource-Based View of the Firm." *Research Policy* 27: 507–523. doi:10.1016/S0048-7333(98)00066-3.

Naman, J. L., and D. P. Slevin. 1993. "Entrepreneurship and the Concept of Fit: A Model and Empirical Tests." *Strategic Management Journal* 14: 137–153. doi:10.1002/(ISSN)1097-0266.

Narula, R. 2004. "R&D Collaboration by Smes: New Opportunities and Limitations in the Face of Globalisation." *Technovation* 24: 153–161. doi:10.1016/S0166-4972(02)00045-7.

Oakey, R. P. 2013. "Open Innovation and Its Relevance to Industrial Research and Development: The Case of High-Technology Small Firms." *International Small Business Journal* 31: 319–336. doi:10.1177/0266242612458942.

Parida, V., M. Westerberg, and J. Frishammar. 2012. "Inbound Open Innovation Activities in High-Tech Smes: The Impact on Innovation Performance." *Journal of Small Business Management* 50: 283–309. doi:10.1111/jsbm.2012.50.issue-2.

Popa, S., P. Soto-Acosta, and I. Martinez-Conesa. 2017. "Antecedents, Moderators, and Outcomes of Innovation Climate and Open Innovation: An Empirical Study in Smes." *Technological Forecasting and Social Change* 118: 134–142. doi:10.1016/j.techfore.2017.02.014.

Remneland Wikhamn, B. 2011. "Open Innovation Climate Measure: The Introduction of a Validated Scale." *Creativity and Innovation Management* 20: 284–295. doi:10.1111/j.1467-8691.2011.00611.x.

Ringle, C. M., and M. Sarstedt. 2016. "Gain More Insight from Your Pls-Sem Results: The Importance-Performance Map Analysis." *Industrial Management & Data Systems* 116: 1865–1886. doi:10.1108/IMDS-10-2015-0449.

Rothwell, R., and M. Dodgson. 1995. "Innovation and Size of Firm." In *TheHandbook of Industrial Innovation*, edited by M. Dodgson and R. Rothwell, 310–324. Aldershot: Edward Elgar Publishing.

Salter, A., P. Criscuolo, and A. L. Ter Wal. 2014. "Coping with Open Innovation: Responding to the Challenges of External Engagement in R&D." *California Management Review* 56: 77–94. doi:10.1525/cmr.2014.56.2.77.

Sarstedt, M., J. Henseler, and C. M. Ringle. 2011. "Multigroup Analysis in Partial Least Squares (Pls) Path Modeling: Alternative Methods and Empirical Results." In *Measurementand Research Methods in International Marketing*, edited by M. Sarstedt, M. Schwaiger, and C. R. Taylor, 195–218. Bingley: Emerald Group Publishing Limited.

Spithoven, A., B. Clarysse, and M. Knockaert. 2011. "Building Absorptive Capacity to Organise Inbound Open Innovation in Traditional Industries." *Technovation* 31: 10–21. doi:10.1016/j.technovation.2010.10.003.

Spithoven, A., W. Vanhaverbeke, and N. Roijakkers. 2013. "Open Innovation Practices in Smes and Large Enterprises." *Small Business Economics* 41: 537–562. doi:10.1007/s11187-012-9453-9.

Teece, D. J. 1986. "Profiting from Technological Innovation: Implications for Integration, Collaboration, Licensing and Public Policy." *Research Policy* 15: 285–305. doi:10.1016/0048-7333(86)90027-2.

Tether, B. S. 2002. "Who Co-Operates for Innovation, and Why: An Empirical Analysis." *Research Policy* 31: 947–967. doi:10.1016/S0048-7333(01)00172-X.

Vanhaverbeke, W., H. Chesbrough, and J. West. 2014. "Surfing the New Wave of Open Innovation Research." In *NewFrontiers in Open Innovation*, edited by H. Chesbrough, W. Vanhaverbeke, and J. West, 278–288. Oxford: Oxford University Press.

Vanhaverbeke, W., F. Frattini, N. Roijakkers, and M. Usman. 2018. *Researching Open Innovation in Smes*. Singapore: World Scientific Publishing Pte..

West, J. 2003. "How Open Is Open Enough?: Melding Proprietary and Open Source Platform Strategies." *Research Policy* 32: 1259–1285. doi:10.1016/S0048-7333(03)00052-0.

West, J., A. Salter, W. Vanhaverbeke, and H. Chesbrough. 2014b. "Open Innovation: The Next Decade." *Research Policy* 43: 805–811. doi:10.1016/j.respol.2014.03.001.

West, J., and M. Bogers. 2014a. "Leveraging External Sources of Innovation: A Review of Research on Open Innovation." *Journal of Product Innovation Management* 31: 814–831. doi:10.1111/jpim.2014.31.issue-4.

West, J., and M. Bogers. 2017. "Open Innovation: Current Status and Research Opportunities." *Innovation* 19: 43–50. doi:10.1080/14479338.2016.1258995.

Zahra, S. A., and G. George. 2002. "Absorptive Capacity: A Review, Reconceptualization, and Extension." *Academy of Management Review* 27: 185–203. doi:10.5465/amr.2002.6587995.

Zobel, A. K. 2017. "Benefiting from Open Innovation: A Multidimensional Model of Absorptive Capacity." *Journal of Product Innovation Management* 34: 269–288. doi:10.1111/jpim.12361.

Zobel, A.-K., B. Lokshin, and J. Hagedoorn. 2017. "Formal and Informal Appropriation Mechanisms: The Role of Openness and Innovativeness." *Technovation* 59: 44–54. doi:10.1016/j.technovation.2016.10.001.

Zynga, A., K. Diener, C. Ihl, D. Lüttgens, F. Piller, and B. Scherb. 2018. "Making Open Innovation Stick: A Study of Open Innovation Implementation in 756 Global Organizations." *Research-Technology Management* 61: 16–25. doi:10.1080/08956308.2018.1471273.

## Appendix Summary of survey questions

| | |
|---|---|
| **Dependent variables** | |
| **Open innovation activity** | |
| **Search breadth (SearchB), Search depth (SearchD)** (0–14), Laursen and Salter (2006) | |
| Search 01 | Universities or other higher education institutes |
| Search 02 | Competitors and other firms from the same industry |
| Search 03 | Government or private non-profit research institutes |
| Search 04 | Commercial laboratories/R&D enterprises/consultants |
| Search 05 | Suppliers of equipment, materials, components or software |
| Search 06 | Clients or customers |
| Search 07 | Professional/industry association and standards organisation |
| Search 08 | Technical/trade press, databases, fairs, and exhibitions |
| Search 09 | Engaging directly with lead users/early adopters |
| Search 10 | Participating in innovation networks/hubs |
| Search 11 | Sharing facilities with other organisations, inventors, etc. |
| Search 12 | CEO meeting, CTO meeting, TMT meeting, etc. |
| Search 13 | Participating in open-source software |
| Search 14 | Exchanging ideas through websites and competitions |
| **Collaboration breadth (CollaboB), Collaboration depth (CollaboD)** (0–7), Laursen and Salter (2006) | |
| Collabo 01 | Universities or other higher education institutes |
| Collabo 02 | Competitors and other firms from the same industry |
| Collabo 03 | Other enterprises within your enterprise group |
| Collabo 04 | Government or private non-profit research institutes |
| Collabo 05 | Commercial laboratories/R&D enterprises/consultants |
| Collabo 06 | Suppliers of equipment, materials, components or software |
| Collabo 07 | Clients or customers |
| **Independent variables** | |
| **Open innovation climate** (1–7), Hung and Chiang (2010) | |
| Climate01 | To profit from an innovation, we need to cooperate with people outside of our company. |
| Climate02 | To profit from an innovation, we need to utilise external ideas to complement the works of our internal R&D department. |
| Climate03 | To profit from an innovation, we need to utilise external ideas that create value for us. |
| Climate04 | To profit from an innovation, we need to originate all the research by ourselves. (reverse coded/ deleted) |
| Climate05 | To profit from an innovation, we need to build a good business model utilising some ideas drawn from outside. |
| Climate06 | To profit from an innovation, we only make use of our internal ideas. (R/deleted) |
| Climate07 | To profit from an innovation, we need to use the intellectual property of others. |
| Climate08 | To profit from an innovation, we allow others to acquire and use our intellectual property. (deleted) |
| **Organisational flexibility** (1–7), Naman and Slevin (1993) | |
| FLEX01 | Open channels of communication with important financial and operating information flowing quite freely throughout the business unit. |
| FLEX02 | Managers' operating styles allowed to range freely from the very formal to the very informal. |
| FLEX03 | A strong tendency to let the expert in a given situation have the most say in decision making, even if this means temporarily bypassing the formal authority. |
| FLEX04 | A strong emphasis on adapting freely to changing circumstances without too much concern for past practice. |
| FLEX05 | A strong emphasis on getting things done even if it means disregarding formal procedures. |

*(Continued)*

(Continued).

| | |
|---|---|
| FLEX06 | Loose, informal control; heavy dependence on informal relationships and norms of cooperation for getting work done. (deleted) |
| FLEX07 | A strong tendency to let the requirements of the situation and the individual's personality define proper on-job behaviour. |
| FLEX08 | The organisational structure is horizontal, and it is possible to explore and reflect on various perspectives. If necessary, flexible changes to the organisation are possible. |
| FLEX09 | Internal collaboration is an important element in the innovation strategy execution. |
| **Entrepreneurial orientation** (1–7), Covin and Slevin (1988) | |
| EO01 | A strong emphasis on R&D, technological leadership, and innovation. |
| EO02 | Over the past three years, there have been many new lines of products or services. |
| EO03 | Over the past three years, there have been quite dramatic changes in product or service lines. |
| EO04 | Our company considers the future to be more important than the present. |
| EO05 | We typically initiate actions to which competitors then respond. |
| EO06 | We are very often the first business to introduce new products/services, administrative techniques operating technologies, etc. |
| EO07 | My business unit typically adopts a very competitive, 'undo-the-competitors' posture. |
| EO08 | My business unit has a strong proclivity for high risk projects (with chances of very high return). |
| EO09 | Owing to the nature of the environment, bold, wide-ranging acts are necessary to achieve the firm's objectives. |
| EO10 | We typically adopt a bold and aggressive posture to maximise the probability of exploiting potential opportunities. |
| **Moderators (organisational facilitators)** | |
| **KMP** (1–7) | We have a patterned process to manage internal R&D outcomes, external collaboration projects, and intellectual property (patents, etc.) (1–7). |
| **KMHR** (1–7) | We have dedicated personnel to manage internal R&D outcomes, external collaboration projects, and intellectual property (patents, etc.) (1–7). |
| **Incentive** (1–7) | Our company provides monetary/non-monetary compensation for actions related to creativity and innovation. |
| **Appropriability** (1–7) | |
| How much of the following method did you use to protect your innovation achievements? (past three years) | |
| **1) Formal appropriability** | |
| FORAPP01 | Copyright/trademarks |
| FORAPP02 | Patent |
| FORAPP03 | Utility model right |
| **2) Informal appropriability** | |
| INFORAPP01 | Non-disclosure agreement |
| INFORAPP02 | Secrecy |
| INFORAPP03 | Complexity of design |
| INFORAPP04 | Lead-time advantage over competitors |

# Internal barriers to innovation and university-industry cooperation among technology-based SMEs in Brazil

Diego R. De Moraes Silva, Luis Otávio Lucas and Nicholas S. Vonortas

**ABSTRACT**

This paper investigates the association between internal barriers to innovation and the propensity of technology-based SMEs to cooperate with universities and research institutes (URIs). We examine empirically two types of internal company barriers – financial and knowledge obstacles to innovation. The data source is the latest edition of the Brazilian Innovation Survey (PINTEC). We analyse the full sample of technology-based SMEs as well as the subsamples of high-tech manufacturing companies and knowledge-intensive business services (KIBS). Financial obstacles are shown to be strongly related to the propensity of KIBS to collaborate with URIs. Knowledge obstacles are moderately related to the propensity of high-tech manufacturing SMEs to collaborate with URIs. We conclude that while URIs have other important roles in the techno-economic system, their perceived contribution to alleviating internal innovation barriers for technology-based SMEs may be less prominent than policy decision-makers in emerging economies may expect.

## 1. Introduction

More than ever before, the dictum 'no firm is an island' (Tidd, Bessant, and Pavitt 2005) rings true nowadays in the innovation realm. Openness and cooperation for innovation have quickly become imperative for many businesses across high-tech sectors. While this is not an entirely new phenomenon (Vonortas 1997; Avellar and Kupfer 2011), it has certainly intensified more recently as transactions and interactions became easier and more widespread due to the diffusion of information and communication technologies, the growing cost and complexity of research and development (R&D) activities, and the advancement of globalisation and liberal political reforms worldwide, among others (Powell and Grodal 2005).

In this context, various countries have developed strong interest in supporting cooperation mechanisms to enhance the innovative performance of firms. If until the end of the century the vast majority of firms involved in cooperation agreements were from developed countries (Hagedoorn 2002; Vonortas and Zirulia 2015), this is rapidly changing. Developing countries and emerging economies have particularly been promoting university-industry cooperation (Freitas, Marques, and Silva 2013; Albuquerque et al. 2015; Moraes Silva, Furtado, and Vonortas 2018). In these countries universities and public research organisations play a key role as 'antennae' linking the country to international flows of science and technology (Kruss et al. 2015).

Connecting the knowledge generated in universities and the flow of well-trained graduates to the productive structure of the economy is understood as a prerequisite for technological and economic development (Mowery and Sampat 2005; Freitas, Marques, and Silva 2013). University-industry interaction has also been seen as a good channel for the creation and strengthen of technology-based small and medium-sized enterprises (SMEs) which rely heavily on external sources to innovate (Tidd, Bessant, and Pavitt 2005; Caetano and Amaral 2011; Protogerou, Caloghirou, and Vonortas 2017). Once again, universities have shown to be notably relevant as source of knowledge for SMEs pursuing innovation in peripheral regions which typically are afflicted by a relative lack of support infrastructure, social capital, access to markets, skilled human resources, etc. (Pinto, Fernandez-Esquinas, and Uyarras 2015).

Our study addresses the association of internal barriers to innovation as perceived by technology-based SMEs with the propensity of these firms to cooperate with universities and research institutes (URIs), using Brazil as a case in point. Innovation requires overcoming obstacles inherent to change and can expose company difficulties with handling internal and external factors (Madrid-Gujarro, Garcia, and Van Auken 2009). As the literature has stressed the importance of internal factors in determining the success or failure of innovation activities of SMEs (Hoffman et al. 1998), we assess the extent to which such companies seek cooperation with URIs to alleviate such constraints within the Brazilian context. Considering the context is of utmost importance since the behaviour of the different actors within a national system of innovation typically varies depending on the development stage of the country under consideration (Arocena and Sutz 2000).

While the bulk of the extant literature has focused on the analysis of obstacles to university-industry cooperation (e.g., López-Martínez et al. 1994; Valentín 2000; Hall, Link, and Scott 2001; Bruneel, D'Este, and Salter 2010), in this paper we study the role played by internal barriers to innovation on the propensity of technology-based SMEs to resort to university-industry partnerships, following the steps of more recent studies (e.g., Antonioli, Marzucchi, and Savona 2017; Kanama and Nishikawa 2017). Therefore, we depart from the general idea that obstacles to innovation do not affect companies' innovative performance directly, but actually make they change their innovation strategy in response to the perception of different barriers. Specifically, we examine the relationship between firm perception of internal barriers to innovation and the company's engagement in cooperation with URIs in order to presumably mitigate some of the effects.

Innovation barriers are typically classified into internal barriers (people- or structure-related, for example) and external barriers (market- or policy context-related, for example). While the external barriers cannot be directly influenced by the company, the internal barriers can be the object of active and direct response by company's decision-makers (Hadjimanolis 2003). Therefore, internal barriers to innovation could be tackled through changes in the innovation strategy of the companies, potentially including cooperative ventures with URIs. We address herein internal innovation barriers related to financial and knowledge constraints. Other internal barriers traditionally found in the literature, such as organisational or management constraints, are omitted from this analysis due to the expectation that URIs cannot contribute significantly to alleviating them.[1]

The Brazilian context is particularly relevant to study this topic for at least two reasons. Firstly, URIs are thought to play a major role in the development process of peripheral regions as they usually concentrate most of the R&D structure and activities in developing countries (Brundenius, Lundvall, and Sutz 2009). For example, according to official data from the Brazilian Ministry of Science, Technology, Innovation and Communication (MCTIC),[2] the R&D expenditure directed to higher education institutions accounted for 62% of the total amount spent on public R&D in 2013. Secondly, policymakers worldwide have been paying increasing attention to technology-based SMEs, which have high innovative potential but also usually face internal resources and capacities shortages that require government intervention (Shapira, Youtie, and Kay 2011). Public policy in Brazil is also following this trend with an expansion of policy instruments to support innovative SMEs via public funding and incentives to collaboration with URIs (Avellar and Botelho 2015).

The empirical investigation is based on recently released dataset from the latest edition of the Brazilian Innovation Survey (PINTEC 2014), carried out by the Brazilian Institute of Geography and Statistics (IBGE). We use PINTEC 2014 microdata which can only be accessed onsite following an elaborate application process designed to ensure the anonymity of responding organisations.[3] Our goal is to study the association between the engagement of technology-based SMEs in cooperative ventures with URIs and these firms' perception of two groups of internal barriers to innovation: financial and knowledge obstacles.

We appraise the association between university-industry cooperation and internal barriers to innovation for the full sample of technology-based SMEs and also separately for the subsamples of high-tech manufacturing companies and knowledge-intensive business services (KIBS). Results show that financial and knowledge obstacles are positively and significantly associated with cooperation with URIs when considering the full sample of technology-based SMEs, but only financial obstacles when both independent variables are included in the econometric model. For the subsample of high-tech manufacturing companies, only knowledge obstacles appear statistically significant in explaining collaboration with URIs, but just when considered separately from financial obstacles. For the subsample of KIBS, only financial obstacles appear strongly statistically significant in explaining collaboration with URIs both when considered separately and jointly with knowledge obstacles in the econometric model.

[1]Organisational barriers were included in earlier versions of this analysis. They were later omitted for statistical reasons. See Section 3.2.

[2]Data accessed at the MCTIC website (www.mctic.gov.br) on July 20th, 2018.

[3]Following international practice, IBGE only publishes aggregate data to guarantee the secrecy of firms' strategic information. In order to use PINTEC's microdata, one needs to follow a formal access procedure involving the submission of a request to access and use the data onsite. Therefore, we do not own the database employed herein, and cannot make it available to other researchers.

The rest of the paper is organised as follows. Section 2 provides the theoretical background and research hypotheses, discussing the relationship between technology-based SMEs and external knowledge exploration, especially via university-industry cooperation, as an alternative to overcome internal barriers to innovation usually faced by these companies, such as those linked to finance and knowledge constraints. Section 3 presents the research design and methodology, and also explains the data. Section 4 discusses the empirical results. Finally, Section 5 provides final remarks and policy implications.

## 2. Theoretical background and hypotheses

### *2.1. Small companies and innovations*

Since the pioneering work by Schumpeter (1942), several authors within the Innovation Studies have built upon the importance of company size in the innovation development, which was later named as the Schumpeterian Hypothesis. The reasoning is straightforward: the larger the company, the higher its internal resources and capacity to explore, on the one hand, economies of scale in research (larger research departments interaction, better ability to exploit specialised equipment, deeper division of labour among researchers) and, on the other, economies of scope in research (name recognition to move easily into new markets, multiproduct approach to deal with diversity) (Kamien and Schwartz 1982; Vonortas 2009a).

However, after several decades of empirical study the validation of the Schumpeterian Hypothesis remains inconclusive, as the findings point out that, although R&D activities increase monotonically with firm size, the number of innovations tends to increase less than proportionally while the share of R&D effort dedicated to more incremental and process innovation expands (Cohen 2010). A new branch of the literature emerged in the 1990s to explain such inconsistencies proposing that smaller firms (small and medium-sized enterprises – SMEs) are more capable of innovating than their larger counterparts, especially when it comes to more radical innovations (Acs and Audretsch 1990; Christensen 1997; Baumol 2002).

Within this new branch, the work by Clayton Christensen (1997) provided one of the most powerful explanations for this situation. He argued that leading, and usually large, companies fail when confronted with disruptive innovations precisely because they are good at working with their mainstream users and incumbent technologies, and then are not able to see the potential of new and typically small markets stemming from cutting-edge technologies. Conversely, smaller companies characteristically possess a range of advantages to tackle the issue of innovations, such as agility, flexibility, openness and fast decision-making (Hoffman et al. 1998).

Nevertheless, small firms differ widely. They account for more than 90% of the private sector in most economies, ranging from mom-and-pop shops to cleaning services to manufacturing firms to information technology and biotechnology start-ups. In this paper we are concerned with a very specific type of SMEs, those based on new technologies, which represent a tiny subset of the overall SME population. We look at companies that have significant knowledge intensity in their activity and exploit innovative opportunities in diverse sectors (Malerba et al. 2016). Such companies are frequently established by highly qualified entrepreneurs, may require significant amounts of capital even at early stages without extensive production capabilities, and are characterised by higher technical and market risk (Tidd, Bessant, and Pavitt 2005).

These companies have been typically named in the literature as technology-based SMEs and have attracted increasing attention as scholars from advanced economies realised the capacity of such firms to reshape the technology and market landscapes (Haeussler, Patzelt, and Zahra 2012). In developing countries, the topic has gained traction more recently (Pinho, Côrtes, and Fernandes 2002; Fernandes, Côrtes, and Pinho 2004; Moraes, Lima, and Lobosco 2011). This paper intends to expand the knowledge about technology-based SMEs in a developing context, exploring the relationship between such companies and universities in the contemporary Brazilian economy.

### 2.2. Technology-based SMEs and external knowledge exploration

There is an extensive amount of literature on inter-organisational collaboration for innovation involving firms, universities, research institutes, and public laboratories stressing the relevance of these relationships to information diffusion, resource sharing, access to specialised assets, and inter-organisational learning (Powell and Grodal 2005; Vanhaverbeke 2006). The need to move away from the idea that innovation stems only (or mostly) from the internal capacities of atomistic economic agents competing for profits in impersonal markets became imperative following the explosion of inter-organisational cooperation during the past four decades and the growing empirical evidence pointing out the importance of networks of collaboration to the innovation process (Vonortas 2009b).

One of the most significant turning points in the literature certainly came from the work by Henry Chesbrough (2003) on Open Innovation, which can basically be understood as the antithesis to the traditional vertical integration model according to which in-house R&D would be the primary driver to internally developed innovations. The Open Innovation approach understands research and technological development as an open system operating in an environment wherein useful knowledge is widely distributed (Chesbrough 2003). Increasing costs and complexity of R&D, the shortening of technology life-cycles, and the rise of markets for technology have challenged the old 'closed innovation' paradigm. Companies stuck at this outdated paradigm are likely to overlook the various business opportunities from the large pool of external knowledge (Vanhaverbeke 2006).

While the Open Innovation paradigm arose precisely to fill this gap, the intention was not to deny the importance of firm internal resources and intramural R&D efforts. On the contrary, since the seminal paper by Cohen and Levinthal (1989) on the dual role of R&D in generating new information, on the one hand, and enhancing firm absorptive capacity to explore external knowledge, on the other, the relevance of the internal capacities of companies has become indisputable, even in an environment of increasing expansion and distribution of the pool of external knowledge. The problem of missed opportunities might be more related to the conservative nature of learning at organisations, resulting in persistent forms of specialisation that can be harmful in environments of constant change (Levinthal 1996). This implies the risk of a 'competence trap' for companies locked in highly specialised technological paths, then losing the ability to appraise external opportunities.

The solution to avoiding the 'competence trap' could presumably be reached through the development of multiple knowledge bases. March (1991) proposed that companies must find an appropriate balance in their innovation search strategies between knowledge exploitation of their current competencies and knowledge exploration of new opportunities. Such notion is in tune with the idea of complementary routines associated with successful innovation management under discontinuous conditions, which tend to be related to highly flexible behaviour, tolerance for ambiguity, and emphasis on fast learning, characteristics often found in small entrepreneurial firms capable of managing innovation in an 'ambidextrous' fashion (Tidd, Bessant, and Pavitt 2005).

Indeed, there is some evidence pointing out that entrepreneurial SMEs might be more likely to have diverse and extensive linkages with a variety of external sources of innovation, thus obtaining necessary resources to develop innovative products and increasing their chance for survival (Powell and Grodal 2005). Freeman and Soete (1997) noticed in their typology of innovation strategies that even though the offensive strategy is usually grounded on a key role for in-house R&D efforts, there is an exception to this generalisation constituted by the small entrepreneurial firms founded in order to explore an innovation partial or totally developed outside their boundaries, especially in the case of technology intensive innovations. These companies are usually involved in so-called strategic technical alliances (or knowledge-intensive partnerships) which are collaborative arrangements focusing primarily on the generation, exchange, adaptation and exploration of technical advances, and typically comprise URIs when R&D is the focus (Rothaermel and Deeds 2006; Vonortas and Zirulia 2015).

It has been frequently pointed out that URIs play a distinctive role in the development of technology-based SMEs. Acs, Audretsch, and Feldman (1994) found that, while large firms are more responsive to intramural R&D than small ones, smaller firms are more responsive to university research than their larger counterparts. The founders of technology-based SMEs frequently have an academic background or even are current or former university employees, so the university researchers may be more willing to work with a small young company which they know the owners rather than faceless large multinational corporations (Storey and Tether 1998). Other studies have pointed out that the presence of URIs in a region favours an enabling environment for the creation of new innovative companies (Fernandes, Côrtes, and Pinho 2004; Fischer, Queiroz, and Vonortas 2018). In fact, it was found in Brazil that technology-based SMEs predominantly cooperate with URIs (more than 50%) instead of other more traditional partners among incumbent companies, such as suppliers (less than 10%) and customers (less than 20%) (Côrtes et al. 2005).

## *2.3. Internal barriers within technology-based SMEs*

The big versatility and ability of technology-based SMEs to explore external knowledge does come with a price. While these companies tend to be less prone to suffer from the 'Not Invented Here' syndrome,[4] the intense openness to external knowledge hinges on

[4]Such syndrome typically involves the inclination of firms to mistrust and not incorporate external knowledge as it does not align with their perception of the technology and industry (Katz and Allen 1982).

their main weaknesses: internal resource deficiencies (Hoffman et al. 1998; Tidd, Bessant, and Pavitt 2005). In fact, sometimes the close links between SMEs and universities imply a lower in-house R&D expenditure (Veugelers and Cassiman 1999), suggesting a substitution of internal capabilities by external ones. The 'Achilles' heel' of technology-based SMEs is precisely their limitation in terms of financial and knowledge internal resources. In a resource-constrained environment, the engagement in cooperative ventures could alleviate the burden of the internal barriers as it expands the firms' knowledge sources and intensifies the generation of new marketable technologies (Pinho, Côrtes, and Fernandes 2002; Kim and Vonortas 2014).

From the perspective of URIs, the motivations to cooperate with companies are various, such as: learning from industry problems, routines and applicability of research; access to in-kind resources such as materials, expertise and equipment; commercialisation of intellectual property and new sources of income; and access to funding from industry or from policy programs to university-industry collaboration (D'Este and Perkmann 2011). Regarding the specifics of the Brazilian case, one must also bear in mind a couple of additional issues. Firstly, in an emerging economy context, universities cannot pick and choose their partners in industry, as they will invariably need to collaborate with firms operating far from the technology frontier (Moraes Silva, Furtado, and Vonortas 2018). Secondly, most initiatives in this context actually come from industry, which seeks URIs collaboration to solve particular problems demanding more in-depth knowledge (Freitas, Marques, and Silva 2013). Therefore, there is no reason to expect URIs to turn down collaboration with firms facing internal barriers; on the contrary, in a developing country context, they are actually expected to contribute for the technological progress of industry and national development (Albuquerque et al. 2015).

The more traditional theoretical perspective on cooperative ventures for innovation has associated incentives to cooperate with learning and knowledge benefits to companies (Mowery and Sampat 2005), but hardly ever with minimising or alleviating their barriers. In turn, the literature on obstacles to innovation has focused on the effect of obstacles on firm innovative performance (Pellegrino and Savona 2017), but has mostly neglected the impact of obstacles in changing company strategy as an indirect effect. Following recent research (e.g., Antonioli, Marzucchi, and Savona 2017; Kanama and Nishikawa 2017), we herein ask whether the perception of internal barriers to innovation by technology-based SMEs fosters cooperative ventures with URIs to alleviate such barriers. In order to tackle this issue, we have formulated the following general research hypotheses based on two recurrent internal barriers as identified in the literature: financial and knowledge obstacles.

Most studies on innovation barriers until recently had focused on financial constraints impact on companies' innovative behaviour based on the seminal works by Nelson (1959) and Arrow (1962) on the (semi) public-good nature of knowledge engendering under-investment in innovation (Hall 2008). The intangible assets produced by knowledge investments may be very difficult to use as collateral in negotiating external funding, since banks prefer physical assets to secure loans and may be reluctant to lend when the project involves the accumulation of intangible assets partially embodied in the firm's personnel (Álvarez and Crespi 2015). Firms pursuing innovation usually face barriers related to economic risk, high cost to innovate and lack of adequate (internal and external) funding. Moreover, it is widely acknowledged that problems associated with financing investments in new (and usually costly) technology are most apparent for small firms and start-ups lacking the appropriate internal funding (Álvarez and Crespi 2015). Smaller firms are more prone to financial constraints as a result of indivisibilities in search costs, shorter track records and less collateral, as well as high-tech companies by their very nature tend to face the same problems plus riskier investments and greater information asymmetry (Canepa and Stoneman 2008). The literature has repeatedly pointed out that external partnerships could help to share costs and risks involved in the innovation process (e.g., Hagedoorn, Link, and Vonortas 2000; Caloghirou, Tsakanikas, and Vonortas 2001; Eom and Lee 2010). Therefore, we hypothesise:

Hypothesis 1 – Technology-based SMEs are more prone to cooperate with URIs when facing financial barriers to innovation;

Recent literature has stressed the importance of knowledge obstacles to innovation, such as lack of qualified personnel and lack of information on technology or markets (D'Este et al. 2012; Pellegrino and Savona 2017). Some studies have found empirical support for the claim that knowledge obstacles might play a significant role in diminishing the propensity of companies to innovate (Segarra-Blasco, Garcia-Quevedo, and Teruel-Carrizosa 2008; Amara et al. 2016). In particular, Galia and Legros (2004) highlight that information on markets and technology is fundamental to the process of matching technology possibilities to market opportunities in the innovation development, while D'Este, Rentocchini, and Vega-Jurado (2014) stress that the breath of firms' skill base is important for innovation particularly within newly established companies and SMEs. In terms of external knowledge sourcing, the decision to collaborate with other actors of the innovation system is usually related to the need to handle internal knowledge and skills shortages as the partnerships might both provide access to crucial knowledge and lead to upgrade of skills (Caloghirou, Ioannides, and Vonortas 2003; Barge-Gil 2010; Antonioli, Marzucchi, and Savona 2017). Therefore, we hypothesise:

Hypothesis 2 – Technology-based SMEs are more prone to cooperate with URIs when facing knowledge barriers to innovation.

## 3. Research design and methodology

### 3.1. Data

Our main data source is the last edition of the Brazilian Innovation Survey (PINTEC 2014), released in late 2016, which was first designed by IBGE in the early 2000s to provide a broad understanding of the innovation and R&D activities in the Brazilian economy and to support the actions and planning of the public and private actors (Moraes Silva and Furtado 2017). PINTEC is similar in structure to the Community Innovation Survey (CIS) in Europe. In line with the third edition of the OECD's Oslo Manual (OECD 2005), the current PINTEC survey covers manufacturing sectors and selected service sectors (notably KIBS) as well as both technological and non-technological innovations (organisational and marketing) (IBGE 2016).

PINTEC 2014 comprises companies that have: i. active status in the Central Business Register held by IBGE; ii. main economic activity in extractive industry, manufacturing industry, electricity and gas, telecommunications, information technology services, architecture and engineering services, R&D services, data processing and web hosting, or editing, printing and music recording; iii. headquarters in Brazil; iv. ten or more employees; v. business entity registration. The survey has two time references: i. most qualitative variables refer to the period 2012–2014; ii. quantitative variables and a few qualitative variables refer to fiscal year 2014.

The survey's sampling design was based on the assumption that innovation is a rare phenomenon. It employed a stratified disproportional sampling procedure in which large companies (more than 500 employees in manufacturing and more than 100 employees in services) were automatically included in the sample while smaller companies were sampled according to their probability of being innovative – more likely innovative companies as identified in a screening process using government databases had higher weight in the sample selection. The final sample reached 17,171 firms, with results expanding to a population of 132,529 firms by means of the Horvitz-Thompson estimator. Table 1 presents the aggregate sectoral distribution of companies surveyed.

PINTEC 2014 covers a wide spectrum of themes, from innovation activities and funding to cooperation partnerships and obstacles to innovation, among others. Figure 1 summarises the sixteen sections of the survey's questionnaire and their directional flow. While a filter mechanism directs non-innovating companies (without ongoing or abandoned projects) to answer a more limited set of sections than innovative ones, both innovators and non-innovators answer the sections on problems and obstacles to innovation, organisational and marketing innovations, and biotechnology and nanotechnology diffusion.

### 3.2. Empirical strategy

This study focuses on technology-based SMEs and subsamples of sectors. We follow the literature to lay emphasis on technology-intensive sectors (Storey and Tether 1998; Haeussler, Patzelt, and Zahra 2012), expecting higher concentration of technology-based SMEs in technologically advanced sectors (Pinho, Côrtes, and Fernandes 2002; Fernandes, Côrtes, and Pinho 2004). Our sample includes companies with 10 to 249 employees (the definition of SMEs in Brazil) in high- and medium-high technology-intensive manufacturing sectors (per the OECD (2011) classification) and in the knowledge-intensive business services sectors (KIBS) surveyed by PINTEC 2014. Table 2 presents the sectors included in our study.

**Table 1.** Distribution of companies surveyed by PINTEC 2014.

| Sector | Total |
|---|---|
| Extractive and manufacturing industries | **14,387** |
| Electricity and gas | **96** |
| Selected services | **2,688** |
| **Total** | **17,171** |

Source: IBGE 2016.

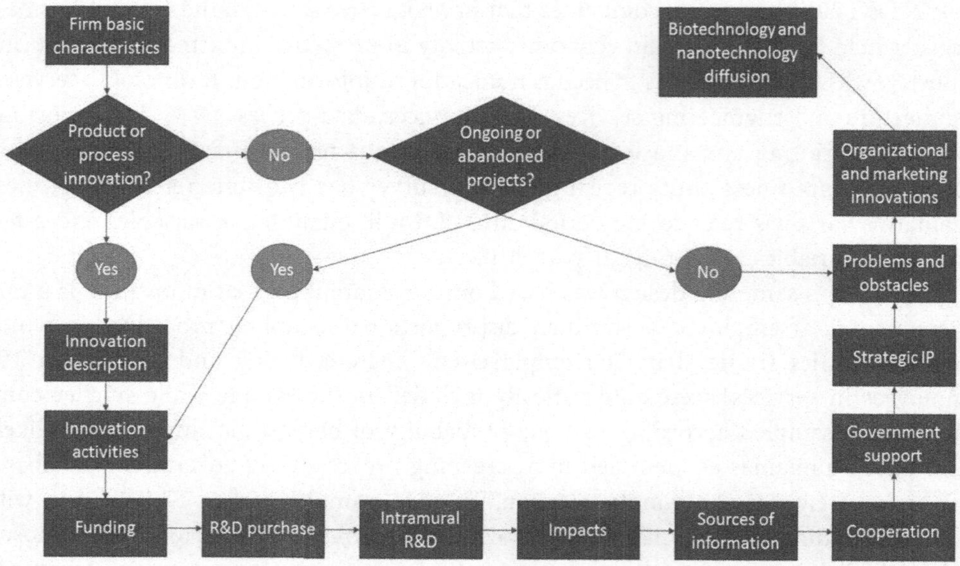


**Figure 1.** Thematic structure from PINTEC 2014.
Source: IBGE 2016.

**Table 2.** Sectors of economic activity.

| Code | Sectors | Technological intensity |
|---|---|---|
| C-20 | Manufacture of chemicals and chemical products | Medium-high |
| C-21 | Manufacture of basic pharmaceutical products and pharmaceutical preparations | High |
| C-26 | Manufacture of computer, electronic and optical products | High |
| C-27 | Manufacture of electrical equipment | Medium-high |
| C-28 | Manufacture of machinery and equipment | Medium-high |
| C-29 | Manufacture of motor vehicles, trailers and semi-trailers | Medium-high |
| C-30 | Manufacture of other transport equipment | Medium-high |
| C-325 | Manufacture of medical and dental instruments and supplies and optical articles | Medium-high |
| J-58 | Press and publishing activities | KIBS |
| J-592 | Sound recording and music publishing activities | KIBS |
| J-61 | Telecommunications | KIBS |
| J-62 | Computer programming, consultancy and related activities | KIBS |
| J-631 | Data processing, web hosting and related activities | KIBS |
| M-71 | Architectural and engineering activities, technical testing and analysis | KIBS |
| M-72 | Scientific research and development | KIBS |

The above selection introduces two important limitations. First, we do not have data on microenterprises (companies with less than 10 employees), even though this type of company may have a significant impact when we talk about knowledge-intensive activities (Baumann and Kritikos 2016). Second, we do not have data on company age, although young firms are often associated with innovativeness when it comes to technology-intensive sectors (Protogerou, Caloghirou, and Vonortas 2017).

We employ econometric analysis to assess the effects of two groups of internal barriers (financial and knowledge) on the propensity of technology-based SMEs to cooperate with URIs in Brazil. We run probit models with the following specification:

$$Prob(Y = 1|x) = \int_{-\infty}^{x'\beta} \phi(t)dt = \Phi(\mathbf{x}'\beta).$$

The set of parameters $\beta$ reflects the impact of changes in **x** on the probability of Y = 1, while the function $\Phi(t)$ is a commonly used notation for the standard normal distribution (Greene 2011). Probit models are appropriate for handling dichotomous dependent variables like our own taking the values one and zero depending on whether companies have or not engaged in cooperative arrangements with universities and research institutes between 2012–2014 (COOPURI).

The independent variables represent a set of internal barriers grouped into two categories: **Financial Obstacles (FINOBS)** including excessive economic risk, high cost to innovate, and lack of adequate funding sources; and **Knowledge Obstacles (KNOBS)** including lack of qualified personnel, lack of information on technology, and lack of information on markets. We have employed a thematic grouping of the various internal barriers. As a robustness check, we ran multiple correspondence analysis to verify whether there would be different or more 'natural' obstacle groups. The analysis did not produce significantly different results, as can be seen in the Appendix Table A1. We also ran Cronbach's Alpha tests to assess the internal consistency and interrelatedness of specific barriers within the aggregate obstacle groups. Both financial and knowledge obstacles appeared fairly consistent, as it can be seen in Appendix Table A2.[5]

All the specific internal barriers' variables are also dummies and indicate whether the company has assigned high importance to such barrier in the period 2012–2014. Basically, companies claiming to have faced innovation barriers were asked to assign importance level (no important, low importance, medium importance, or high importance) to twelve different obstacles to innovation listed in the survey. The six barriers included in this study are those more typically considered as internal and related to companies' willingness to cooperate with URIs, while three omitted are more related to organisational and regulation issues (organisational rigidities, innovation centralised in another company from the same corporate group, and difficulty to comply with norms, standards and regulations), which might be considered internal but not directly linked to the propensity to cooperate with URIs, and the other three omitted (scant possibilities to cooperate, lack of demand, and lack of external technical services) are those more typically considered as external barriers.

The aggregate independent variables (FINOBS and KNOBS) were constructed to indicate whether the company has assigned high importance to at least one of the internal barriers comprised in each group. In short, then, financial obstacles refer to the perception of either a risky economic environment limiting the innovative enterprise, or high costs for engaging in innovation activities, or difficulties to access adequate funding for that purpose, or even a combination of these issues; knowledge obstacles, on the other hand, refer to either a lack of techno-scientific information to develop an innovation, or a lack of market information to properly commercialise the innovation, or a lack of knowledge embodied in skilled personnel working on innovation activities, or finally a combination of these barriers.

[5]Appendix Tables A1 and A2 include a group of organisational obstacles as well since, at first, we had considered including these barriers in the analysis. As it can be observed, however, consistency of these barriers was lacking, underlining the decision to omit them.

As another robustness check, we ran models with an alternative measure of the independent variables (named FINOBS2 and KNOBS2, respectively) to verify whether the particular operationalisation drives the results. Instead of dummy variables, we operationalised the independent variables as ranging from 0 (none of the specific barriers was highly important) to 3 (all three specific barriers were highly important). The results showed more statistically significant coefficients (see Appendix Tables A3, A4 and A5), mostly reinforcing the importance of the financial obstacles across the models. This was not surprising given that descriptive statistics indicate they are far more prevalent, so a variable that measures obstacles intensity rather than merely absence or presence naturally reveals that. However, our conceptual interest herein lies more on measuring the absence or presence of internal barriers instead of their intensity, so we stick to the original operationalisation.

We also include a set of controls to account for other factors that likely impact on firms' propensity to cooperate with URIs, reducing potential omitted variable bias. First, a dummy variable indicating high expenditure (above the sample average) on intramural R&D (HRD) accounting for the companies' absorptive capacity (Laursen and Salter 2004). Second, a dummy variable indicating the introduction of product or process innovation at country or world level (INNO) approximating firm innovativeness (Kim and Vonortas 2014). Third, a dummy variable indicating whether the company is part of a corporate group (GRP) (Tether 2002). Fourth, a dummy variable indicating the use of informal methods of intellectual property protection (IMP) (Eom and Lee 2010). Fifth, a dummy variable indicating the use of policy instruments supporting innovation activities (GOV) to account for public policy support (Negassi 2004). Finally, we also introduced dummy variables for each macro-region of the country (South, Southeast, North, Northeast and Central-West) accounting for regional particularities and dummy variables for each sector of economic activity controlling for sectoral heterogeneity. Hence, we have the following general specification for our models:

$$COOPURI_i = \alpha + \beta_1 OBS_i + \beta_2 X_i + \varepsilon_i$$

where COOPURI denotes the dependent variable, OBS is a vector of the explanatory variables grouping the different internal barriers as perceived by companies (FINOBS and KNOBS), X is a vector of control variables, and ε is the error term. In addition to the coefficients, we report the marginal effects of the probit models as well. Table 3 presents the list of variables.

We run two specifications of the model. First, we run the model for the whole sample of technology-based SMEs. Second, we also run the model separately for two subsamples differentiating between manufacturing and service sectors expecting significant differences among them due to sectoral particularities (Gallouj and Savona 2009).

## 4. Results and discussion

### 4.1. Descriptive statistics

As shown in Table 4, we work with a fairly balanced sectoral distribution of firms – about 2,000 firms belonging to manufacturing high-tech sectors and 1,700 belonging to KIBS – and a slightly less balanced size distribution – the number of medium-sized

**Table 3.** List of variables.

| Variable | Description |
|---|---|
| COOPURI | Cooperation partnership with universities or research institutes |
| FINOBS | Assignment of high importance to at least one financial obstacle to innovation (excessive economic risk, high cost to innovate, lack of adequate funding sources) |
| KNOBS | Assignment of high importance to at least one knowledge obstacle to innovation (lack of qualified personnel, lack of information on technology, lack of information on markets) |
| HRD | High expenditure (above the sample average) on intramural R&D in 2014 |
| INNO | Introduction of product or process innovation at the country or world level |
| GRP | Affiliation to a national or international corporate group |
| IMP | Use of at least one informal method of intellectual property protection (product design complexity, industrial secrecy, lead time over competitors, among others) |
| GOV | Use of at least one policy instrument (tax breaks, subsidies, public procurement, public funding and venture capital, among others) for supporting innovation activities |

* All variables are dummies and defined over the reference period 2012–2014, unless when specified differently.

**Table 4.** Sample characterisation.

| Size/Sector | High-tech | KIBS | Total |
|---|---|---|---|
| Small (10–49 employees) | 733 | 746 | **1,479** |
| Medium (50–249 employees) | 1,312 | 945 | **2,257** |
| **Total** | **2,045** | **1,691** | **3,736** |

companies in the sample is about 50% larger than the number of small companies. The total sample is made of 3,736 firms.

Company response distribution in terms of assigned importance to the obstacles addressed in this study is shown in Table 5. This table presents the number of firms according to size strata and sector groups assigning high importance to the aggregates of internal barriers. It can be observed that financial obstacles receive the highest mention across all firm sizes and sectors. Medium-sized firms and high-tech manufacturing firms assign higher importance across all types of obstacles. However, one needs to keep in mind that the intersection of these two groups (1,312 firms) comprises more than one third of the total sample.

A more disaggregated look is offered in Table 6 which presents the number of companies from different size and sectoral sets assigning high importance to the specific internal barriers. The data shows that the most consistent barrier across different sizes and sectors is the high cost to innovate, followed by excessive economic risk – thus demonstrating once again the predominance of financial obstacles to innovation among technology-based SMEs. Within the group of knowledge obstacles, the most important barrier is the lack of qualified personnel.

Table 7 shows the distribution of firm responses as regards the control variables. Once again one can observe high concentration in the group of medium-sized and manufacturing high-tech companies. Comparing the data from Tables 5 and 7 indicates that the same group of companies (medium-sized high-tech manufacturing) more

**Table 5.** Aggregate obstacles response distribution.

| | Size | | Sector | |
|---|---|---|---|---|
| Obstacles to innovation | Small firms | Medium firms | High-tech | KIBS |
| Financial obstacles | 460 | 743 | 706 | 497 |
| Knowledge obstacles | 223 | 294 | 300 | 217 |

**Table 6.** Specific barriers response distribution.

| | Size | | Sector | |
|---|---|---|---|---|
| Obstacles to innovation | Small firms | Medium firms | High-tech | KIBS |
| Excessive economic risk | 322 | 482 | 489 | 315 |
| High cost to innovate | 353 | 553 | 527 | 379 |
| Lack of adequate funding sources | 270 | 373 | 384 | 259 |
| Lack of qualified personnel | 172 | 211 | 208 | 175 |
| Lack of information on technology | 78 | 93 | 109 | 62 |
| Lack of information on markets | 72 | 94 | 101 | 65 |

**Table 7.** Control response distribution.

| | Small firms | | Medium firms | |
|---|---|---|---|---|
| Control variables | High-tech | KIBS | High-tech | KIBS |
| High R&D | 35 | 55 | 289 | 178 |
| Innovativeness | 89 | 69 | 305 | 156 |
| Informal IP | 131 | 95 | 480 | 184 |
| Government support | 107 | 82 | 322 | 153 |
| Group affiliation | 53 | 75 | 237 | 185 |

intensively reporting internal obstacles to innovation is also the one more engaged in innovation-related activities. This seems consistent with recent literature pointing out that companies need to pursue innovation in order to face barriers (D'Este et al. 2012). The most frequently mentioned factor is the use of informal methods of intellectual property protection (complexity of product design, industrial secrecy, time lead over competitors, etc.).

Finally, Table 8 contains the descriptive statistics on means, standard deviations and correlations between the explanatory and control variables. It displays low values of both means and standard deviations. The correlation matrix indicates no correlation higher than 50% and, thus, no concern for multicollinearity.

### 4.2. Estimation results

The next three Tables present the estimation results. Table 9 presents the results for the full sample of technology-based SMEs, Table 10 presents the results for the subsample of high-tech manufacturing firms, and Table 11 presents the results for the subsample of KIBS firms. Each table comprises four models. The first model includes only the control variables as a baseline model, the second adds the financial obstacles (FINOBS) only, the third adds the knowledge obstacles (KNOBS) only, and the fourth model adds

**Table 8.** Descriptive statistics (means and standard deviations) and correlation matrix of explanatory and control variables ($n$ = 3,736).

| Variable | Mean | S.D. | 1 | 2 | 3 | 4 | 5 | 6 | 7 |
|---|---|---|---|---|---|---|---|---|---|
| 1. FINOBS | 0.322 | 0.467 | 1 | | | | | | |
| 2. KNOBS | 0.138 | 0.345 | 0.404 | 1 | | | | | |
| 3. HRD | 0.149 | 0.356 | 0.145 | 0.093 | 1 | | | | |
| 4. INNO | 0.165 | 0.371 | 0.141 | 0.094 | 0.389 | 1 | | | |
| 5. IMP | 0.238 | 0.426 | 0.184 | 0.147 | 0.339 | 0.401 | 1 | | |
| 6. GOV | 0.177 | 0.382 | 0.151 | 0.121 | 0.373 | 0.267 | 0.321 | 1 | |
| 7. GRP | 0.147 | 0.354 | −0.031 | −0.028 | 0.097 | 0.079 | 0.054 | 0.055 | 1 |

**Table 9.** Probit regression results (Full sample: $n$ = 3,736 firms).

| | Model 1 | | Model 2 | | Model 3 | | Model 4 | |
|---|---|---|---|---|---|---|---|---|
| Variables | Coefficients | Marginal effects | Coefficients | Marginal effects | Coefficients | Marginal effects | Coefficients | Marginal effects |
| FINOBS | | | 0.209*** | 0.020*** | | | 0.171** | 0.016** |
| | | | (0.076) | (0.007) | | | (0.081) | (0.007) |
| KNOBS | | | | | 0.207** | 0.020** | 0.135 | 0.013 |
| | | | | | (0.091) | (0.008) | (0.097) | (0.009) |
| GOV | 0.546*** | 0.053*** | 0.532*** | 0.051*** | 0.533*** | 0.051*** | 0.527*** | 0.051*** |
| | (0.083) | (0.008) | (0.083) | (0.008) | (0.084) | (0.008) | (0.084) | (0.008) |
| INNO | 0.358*** | 0.035*** | 0.349*** | 0.033*** | 0.353*** | 0.034*** | 0.348*** | 0.033*** |
| | (0.087) | (0.008) | (0.087) | (0.008) | (0.087) | (0.008) | (0.087) | (0.008) |
| HRD | 0.661*** | 0.064*** | 0.648*** | 0.062*** | 0.661*** | 0.064*** | 0.650*** | 0.063*** |
| | (0.088) | (0.008) | (0.088) | (0.008) | (0.088) | (0.008) | (0.088) | (0.008) |
| GRP | 0.200** | 0.019** | 0.218** | 0.021** | 0.212** | 0.020** | 0.223** | 0.021** |
| | (0.094) | (0.009) | (0.094) | (0.009) | (0.094) | (0.009) | (0.094) | (0.009) |
| IMP | 0.439*** | 0.042*** | 0.417*** | 0.040*** | 0.424*** | 0.041*** | 0.411*** | 0.039*** |
| | (0.083) | (0.008) | (0.083) | (0.008) | (0.083) | (0.008) | (0.083) | (0.008) |
| Sectoral dummies | YES | YES | YES | YES | YES | YES | YES | YES |
| Regional dummies | YES | YES | YES | YES | YES | YES | YES | YES |
| Constant | −1.947*** | | −2.036*** | | −1.937*** | | −2.013*** | |
| | (0.494) | | (0.499) | | (0.494) | | (0.243) | |
| Observations | 3,736 | 3,736 | 3,736 | 3,736 | 3,736 | 3,736 | 3,736 | 3,736 |
| Pseudo $R^2$ | 0.239 | | 0.243 | | 0.242 | | 0.244 | |

*** $p < 0.01$. ** $p < 0.05$. * $p < 0.1$; Standard errors in parentheses.

**Table 10.** Probit regression results (High-tech manufacturing: $n = 2{,}045$ firms).

| | Model 5 | | Model 6 | | Model 7 | | Model 8 | |
|---|---|---|---|---|---|---|---|---|
| Variables | Coefficient | Marginal effects | Coefficient | Marginal effects | Coefficient | Marginal effects | Coefficient | Marginal effects |
| FINOBS | | | 0.146 | 0.014 | | | 0.091 | 0.008 |
| | | | (0.104) | (0.010) | | | (0.110) | (0.010) |
| KNOBS | | | | | 0.247** | 0.024** | 0.212 | 0.020 |
| | | | | | (0.124) | (0.012) | (0.130) | (0.012) |
| GOV | 0.569*** | 0.056*** | 0.566*** | 0.055*** | 0.566*** | 0.055*** | 0.565*** | 0.055*** |
| | (0.108) | (0.010) | (0.109) | (0.010) | (0.109) | (0.010) | (0.109) | (0.010) |
| INNO | 0.361*** | 0.035*** | 0.356*** | 0.035*** | 0.363*** | 0.035*** | 0.360*** | 0.035*** |
| | (0.113) | (0.011) | (0.114) | (0.011) | (0.114) | (0.011) | (0.114) | (0.011) |
| HRD | 0.777*** | 0.076*** | 0.771*** | 0.075*** | 0.776*** | 0.075*** | 0.772*** | 0.075*** |
| | (0.114) | (0.011) | (0.114) | (0.011) | (0.109) | (0.011) | (0.114) | (0.011) |
| GRP | 0.350*** | 0.034*** | 0.362*** | 0.035*** | 0.365*** | 0.035*** | 0.371*** | 0.036*** |
| | (0.124) | (0.012) | (0.124) | (0.012) | (0.124) | (0.012) | (0.125) | (0.012) |
| IMP | 0.475*** | 0.046*** | 0.456*** | 0.044*** | 0.446*** | 0.043*** | 0.438*** | 0.042*** |
| | (0.110) | (0.010) | (0.111) | (0.010) | (0.112) | (0.010) | (0.112) | (0.011) |
| Sectoral dummies | YES | YES | YES | YES | YES | YES | YES | YES |
| Regional dummies | YES | YES | YES | YES | YES | YES | YES | YES |
| Constant | −2.508*** | | −2.586*** | | −2.549*** | | −2.593*** | |
| | (0.407) | | (0.417) | | (0.407) | | (0.378) | |
| Observations | 2,045 | 2,045 | 2,045 | 2,045 | 2,045 | 2,045 | 2,045 | 2,045 |
| Pseudo $R^2$ | 0.300 | | 0.302 | | 0.304 | | 0.304 | |

*** $p < 0.01$. ** $p < 0.05$. * $p < 0.1$; Standard errors in parentheses.

**Table 11.** Probit regression results (KIBS: $n = 1{,}691$ firms).

| | Model 9 | | Model 10 | | Model 11 | | Model 12 | |
|---|---|---|---|---|---|---|---|---|
| Variables | Coefficients | Marginal effects | Coefficients | Marginal effects | Coefficients | Marginal effects | Coefficients | Marginal effects |
| FINOBS | | | 0.334*** | 0.030*** | | | 0.329*** | 0.030*** |
| | | | (0.115) | (0.010) | | | (0.124) | (0.011) |
| KNOBS | | | | | 0.170 | 0.015 | 0.019 | 0.001 |
| | | | | | (0.140) | (0.013) | (0.151) | (0.014) |
| GOV | 0.525*** | 0.049*** | 0.477*** | 0.044*** | 0.499*** | 0.046*** | 0.475*** | 0.043*** |
| | (0.135) | (0.012) | (0.136) | (0.012) | (0.137) | (0.012) | (0.137) | (0.012) |
| INNO | 0.371*** | 0.034*** | 0.349** | 0.032** | 0.359** | 0.033** | 0.348** | 0.032** |
| | (0.140) | (0.013) | (0.141) | (0.013) | (0.140) | (0.012) | (0.141) | (0.013) |
| HRD | 0.467*** | 0.043*** | 0.443*** | 0.040*** | 0.472*** | 0.044*** | 0.444*** | 0.041*** |
| | (0.144) | (0.013) | (0.144) | (0.013) | (0.144) | (0.013) | (0.144) | (0.013) |
| GRP | 0.025 | 0.002 | 0.054 | 0.005 | 0.033 | 0.003 | 0.055 | 0.005 |
| | (0.153) | (0.014) | (0.154) | (0.014) | (0.154) | (0.014) | (0.154) | (0.014) |
| IMP | 0.422*** | 0.039*** | 0.405*** | 0.037*** | 0.421*** | 0.039*** | 0.405*** | 0.037*** |
| | (0.132) | (0.012) | (0.132) | (0.012) | (0.131) | (0.012) | (0.132) | (0.012) |
| Sectoral dummies | YES | YES | YES | YES | YES | YES | YES | YES |
| Regional dummies | YES | YES | YES | YES | YES | YES | YES | YES |
| Constant | −1.227** | | −1.291** | | −1.202** | | −1.287** | |
| | (0.555) | | (0.318) | | (0.319) | | (0.320) | |
| Observations | 1,691 | 1,691 | 1,691 | 1,691 | 1,691 | 1,691 | 1,691 | 1,691 |
| Pseudo $R^2$ | 0.176 | | 0.188 | | 0.178 | | 0.188 | |

*** $p < 0.01$. ** $p < 0.05$. * $p < 0.1$; Standard errors in parentheses.

both independent variables to the baseline model. We can thus assess how much additional variance the independent variables explain in our models.

In Table 9 (full sample) all the independent variables are positively and significantly associated with the tendency of technology-based SMEs to cooperate with URIs when separately included in the models, but only 'Financial Obstacles' (FINOBS) presents a strong association. However, when the two variables are jointly included in Model 4, only FINOBS displays a statistically significant coefficient. The Pseudo $R^2$ values show that the goodness of fit of the models slightly improves with the addition of the independent variables in comparison to the baseline model including only the control variables.

In Table 10 (high-tech manufacturing subsample) only 'Knowledge Obstacles' (KNOBS) is positively and significantly associated with the tendency of technology-based SMEs to cooperate with URIs when separately included in the models, although it does not display a very strong association. With the join inclusion of all independent variables in Model 8, none of them presents statistically significant coefficients. Once again, the Pseudo $R^2$ values reveal a minor improvement of the goodness of fit with the inclusion of the independent variables in comparison to the baseline model.

Finally, in Table 11 (KIBS subsample) only 'Financial Obstacles' (FINOBS) presents positive and statistically significant associations with the dependent variable when separately included in the models. When the independent variables are jointly included in Model 12, the coefficient of FINOBS keeps its strong statistical significance while the other independent variable displays a statistically insignificant coefficient. Once again, we can observe through the Pseudo $R^2$ values a slight improvement in the goodness of fit of the models with the inclusion of the independent variables. By and large, the control variables had the expected positive and significant coefficients across all models' specifications and samples.

On the whole, the estimation results reported above lead to the following overall observations:

(1) Financial obstacles appear moderately linked to university-industry cooperation in the case of the full sample of technology-based SMEs and strongly linked in the case of the subsample of knowledge-intensive business services SMEs. While the literature has identified cooperative ventures in general as an important coping strategy to share costs, risks and to reduce the financial burden between partners, cooperation with universities appears in our analysis strongly and positively linked only to business services when the sample of technology-based SMEs is disaggregated by sector. Thus, hypothesis 1 is only partially confirmed.

(2) Knowledge obstacles appear moderately linked to university-industry cooperation in the cases of the full sample of technology-based SMEs and the subsample of high-tech manufacturing SMEs, but only when included separately in the models. While the literature has identified the relevance of cooperative arrangements in general to explore external knowledge and cope with internal knowledge shortages, the presumed knowledge transfer here is certainly preconditioned upon a minimum level of internal absorptive capacity in terms of skills and knowledge base. Technology-based SMEs are naturally expected to

have such capacity, which could explain why knowledge barriers are not strongly linked to collaboration with universities and appear significant only when Financial Obstacles are not included in the models. When the full sample is disaggregated by sector, knowledge obstacles appear to associate only with high-tech manufacturing SMEs. Therefore, hypothesis 2 is only partially confirmed.

(3) The control variables appear highly statistically significant in their association to cooperation between URIs and technology-based SMEs across the different sectoral groups. Elements such as company innovativeness, R&D expenditure, group affiliation, public support, and use of informal intellectual property protection instruments were strongly associated to company propensity to engage in cooperative ventures with URIs. The only exception is group affiliation for the subsample of KIBS, which did not display any statistically significant coefficient.

## 5. Final remarks and policy implications

This paper appraised the relationship between internal firm barriers to innovation and the propensity of technology-based SMEs to engage in university-industry cooperation. Our analysis was motivated by arguments in recent literature stressing that companies change their strategy in response to their perception of innovation obstacles, and that cooperative ventures with other organisations may provide an alternative (Antonioli, Marzucchi, and Savona 2017). Relying on microdata from the sixth edition of the Brazilian Innovation Survey (PINTEC 2014), we empirically investigated this issue in the context of an emerging economy.

In the case of the full sample of technology-based SMEs, only the perception of financial obstacles was found to be positively and significantly associated with the probability of firms engaging in cooperative ventures with URIs when both independent variables were included in the econometric model. By and large, collaborating with URIs and thus accessing public funds more easily can certainly be a strong incentive for SMEs. Access to expensive, modern technological infrastructure of well-funded research groups in URIs can provide yet another strong incentive. However, we found results somewhat different when we split the sample of technology-based SMEs between the subsamples of high-tech manufacturing and KIBS.

In the case of high-tech manufacturing companies, only knowledge obstacles are associated with cooperative ventures with URIs, and only when considered separately from financial obstacles. As manufacturing companies are probably more engaged in science-based activities than the ones operating in services, the need to resort to university-industry collaborations in order to access basic research and specialised equipment might be bigger. External knowledge exploration is evidently one of the tenets for university-industry cooperation, since the knowledge produced by URIs is usually of a more fundamental nature than what industry does and, to the extent it is useful for business purposes, industry will try to establish channels for collaboration and learning. But, as we can see from the results, we found only a weak association for this variable, raising questions on the capacity of university-industry cooperation to mitigate internal knowledge constraints from technology-based SMEs.

In the case of KIBS, the financial obstacles are strongly associated with cooperation with URIs both when considered solely and jointly with knowledge obstacles in the econometric model. This is the most significant result that we found from our statistical estimations. For service companies, it is crystal clear that sharing research costs and accessing public funding appear to be the primary incentives for collaboration. In fact, companies operating in the services sector are known to suffer from more severe financial constraints than those in manufacturing. Thus, the company strategy of relying on cooperative ventures with URIs to mitigate financial barriers to innovation might be more reasonable for KIBS as these are a more pronounced issue for them.

Our general results overall tend to indicate that university-industry cooperation is not an efficient strategy for technology-based SMEs to overcome internal barriers. That, of course, should not be taken to imply that industry cooperation with URIs is not important in developing countries. What it says is that such cooperation is not perceived by technology-based SMEs to be of critical importance in alleviating internal innovation obstacles. This may, in fact, not be surprising – it corroborates survey results around the world that have repeatedly shown SMEs rating collaboration with universities quite low in their strategic outlook. The reason is simple: URIs are not typically geared up to short- and medium-term innovation, the typical timeframe of technology-based SMEs, and short of funds. While universities and research institutes have other very important roles in our techno-economic systems – as, for instance, is indicated by the strong association with high innovativeness and R&D expenditure in our empirical investigation – their perceived contribution in alleviating internal barriers to innovation for technology-based SMEs in a developing economy may not be among their top contributions.

From the policy perspective, these findings suggest that creating public incentives for technology-based SMEs to cooperate with URIs is not the best strategy to help these companies overcome internal barriers to innovation. The obtained results showed that such cooperative ventures are unlikely to mitigate internal barriers. One possible exception refers to financial obstacles among technology-based SMEs operating in KIBS. In this case, university-industry cooperation was consistently and strongly associated to financial constraints, although the marginal effect of the relationship was fairly low (about 3%). Since the predominant barriers among technology-based SMEs are of financial nature, public policy should focus on tackling this issue not necessarily via university-industry cooperation but mostly through creating specific business lines of credit and venture capital to these firms or improving the broad economic environment in order to reduce the cost to engage in innovation activities.

Future work should try to correct some of the limitations of this analysis. First, cross-sectional models cannot control for unobserved and time-invariant heterogeneity across firms. Therefore, the fact that our models are limited to a single time observation implies that we cannot claim causality, but only statistical associations between the dependent and independent variables. One possible way of overcoming this limitation would be to run panel models using more than one edition of PINTEC. The challenge here is that the variables and scope of PINTEC have changed over time. Second, PINTEC data do not include important information such as company age, manager profile, team culture, patents, and micro-enterprises. Company age, in particular, might significantly correlate with the internal barriers, but the challenge here is in merging PINTEC data with other surveys, which is far from simple since only IBGE owns the database and might authorise and undertake this type of procedure. Third, the analysis should be replicated with similar data in other emerging economies in order to be able to compare across countries and start addressing the effect of systemic factors on the relationships examined herein.

## Acknowledgments

A preliminary version of this paper was presented at the DRUID Conference, Copenhagen, June 2018; we are grateful to the discussants for insightful remarks. We would also like to thank the two anonymous referees and the guest editors of this Journal for their helpful and detailed comments, as well as the IBGE for providing access to the microdata from PINTEC. The authors acknowledge support by the São Paulo Research Foundation (FAPESP) in connection to the São Paulo Excellence Chair in Innovation Systems, Strategy and Policy (InSySPo) established at the University of Campinas (UNICAMP). Diego de Moraes Silva and Luis Lucas acknowledge support of CAPES doctoral scholarships and the infrastructural support by UNICAMP's Department of Science and Technology Policy. Nicholas Vonortas acknowledges the infrastructural support of the Institute for International Science and Technology Policy at the George Washington University. He also acknowledges support from the Basic Research Program at the National Research University Higher School of Economics within the framework of the subsidy to the HSE by the Russian Academic Excellence Project '5–100'. None of these organisations is responsible for the contents of this paper. Remaining mistakes and misconceptions are solely the responsibility of the authors.

## Disclosure statement

No potential conflict of interest was reported by the authors.

## ORCID

Diego R. De Moraes Silva http://orcid.org/0000-0003-3615-8873

## References

Acs, Z., and D. Audretsch. 1990. *Innovation and Small Firms*. Cambridge: MIT Press.

Acs, Z., D. Audretsch, and M. Feldman. 1994. "R&D Spillovers and Recipient Firm Size." *Review of Economics and Statistics* 76: 336–340. doi:10.2307/2109888.

Albuquerque, E., W. Suzigan, G. Kruss, and K. Lee. 2015. *Developing National Systems of Innovation: University-Industry Interactions in the Global South*. Cheltenham: Edward Elgar.

Álvarez, R., and G. Crespi. 2015. "Heterogeneous Effects of Financial Constraints on Innovation: Evidence from Chile." *Science and Public Policy* 42 (5): 711–724. doi:10.1093/scipol/scu091.

Amara, N., P. D'Este, R. Landry, and D. Doloreux. 2016. "Impacts of Obstacles on Innovation Patterns in KIBS Firms." *Journal of Business Research* 69: 4065–4073. doi:10.1016/j.jbusres.2016.03.045.

Antonioli, D., A. Marzucchi, and M. Savona. 2017. "Pain Shared, Pain Halved? Cooperation as a Coping Strategy for Innovation Barriers." *The Journal of Technology Transfer* 42 (4): 841–864. doi:10.1007/s10961-016-9545-9.

Arocena, R., and J. Sutz. 2000. "Looking at National Systems of Innovation from the South." *Industry and Innovation* 7 (1): 55–75. doi:10.1080/713670247.

Arrow, K. 1962. "The Economic Implications of Learning by Doing." *Review of Economic Studies* 29: 155–173. doi:10.2307/2295952.

Avellar, A., and M. Botelho. 2015. "Políticas de apoio à inovação em pequenas empresas: Evidências sobre a experiência brasileira recente." *Economia e Sociedade* 24 (2): 379–417. doi:10.1590/1982-3533.2015v24n2art6.

Avellar, A., and D. Kupfer. 2011. "Innovation and Cooperation: Evidence from the Brazilian Innovation Survey." In *National Innovation Surveys in Latin America: Empirical Evidence and Policy Implications*, edited by the Economic Comission for Latin America and the Caribbean (ECLAC), 31–51. Santiago, Chile: ECLAC – Project documents collection.

Barge-Gil, A. 2010. "Cooperation-Based Innovators and Peripheral Cooperators: An Empirical Analysis of Their Characteristics and Behavior." *Technovation* 30: 195–206. doi:10.1016/j.technovation.2009.11.004.

Baumann, J., and A. Kritikos. 2016. "The Link between R&D, Innovation and Productivity: Are Micro Firms Different?" *Research Policy* 45: 1263–1274. doi:10.1016/j.respol.2016.03.008.

Baumol, W. 2002. *The Free-Market Innovation Machine*. Princeton: Princeton University Press.

Brundenius, C., B.-A. Lundvall, and J. Sutz. 2009. "The Role of Universities in Innovation Systems in Developing Countries: Developmental University System – Empirical, Analytical and Normative Perspectives." In *Handbook of Innovation Systems and Developing Countries*, edited by B. -A. Lundvall, K. J. Joseph, C. Chaminade and J. Vang, 311–335. Cheltenham: Edward Elgar.

Bruneel, J., P. D'Este, and A. Salter. 2010. "Investigating the Factors that Diminish the Barriers to University-Industry Collaboration." *Research Policy* 39: 858–868. doi:10.1016/j.respol.2010.03.006.

Caetano, M., and D. Amaral. 2011. "Roadmapping for Technology Push and Partnership: A Contribution for Open Innovation Environments." *Technovation* 31 (7): 320–335. doi:10.1016/j.technovation.2011.01.005.

Caloghirou, Y., S. Ioannides, and N. Vonortas. 2003. "Research Joint Ventures." *Journal of Economic Surveys* 17: 541–570. doi:10.1111/1467-6419.00204.

Caloghirou, Y., A. Tsakanikas, and N. Vonortas. 2001. "University-Industry Cooperation in the Context of the European Framework Programmes." *The Journal of Technology Transfer* 26: 153–161. doi:10.1023/A:1013025615518.

Canepa, A., and P. Stoneman. 2008. "Financial Constraints to Innovation in the UK: Evidence from CIS2 and CIS3." *Oxford Economic Papers* 60: 711–730. doi:10.1093/oep/gpm044.

Chesbrough, H. 2003. *Open Innovation: The New Imperative for Creating and Profiting from Technology*. Boston: Harvard Business School Press.

Christensen, C. 1997. *The Innovator's Dilemma: When New Technologies Cause Great Firms to Fail*. Boston: Harvard Business School Press.

Cohen, W. 2010. "Fifty Years of Empirical Studies of Innovative Activity and Performance." In *Handbook of the Economics of Innovation*, edited by B. Hall and N. Rosenberg, 129–213. Amsterdam: Elsevier.

Cohen, W., and D. Levinthal. 1989. "Innovation and Learning: The Two Faces of R&D." *The Economic Journal* 99: 569–596. doi:10.2307/2233763.

Côrtes, M., M. Pinho, A. Fernandes, R. Smolka, and A. Barreto. 2005. "Cooperação em empresas de base tecnológica: Uma primeira avaliação baseada numa pesquisa abrangente." *São Paulo em Perspectiva* 19 (1): 85–94. doi:10.1590/S0102-88392005000100007.

D'Este, P., S. Iammarino, M. Savona, and N. von Tunzelman. 2012. "What Hampers Innovation? Revealed Barriers versus Deterring Barriers." *Research Policy* 41: 482–488. doi:10.1016/j.respol.2011.09.008.

D'Este, P., and M. Perkmann. 2011. "Why Do Academics Engage with Industry? the Entrepreneurial University and Individual Motivations." *The Journal of Technology Transfer* 36 (3): 316–339. doi:10.1007/s10961-010-9153-z.

D'Este, P., F. Rentocchini, and J. Vega-Jurado. 2014. "The Role of Human Capital in Lowering the Barriers to Engaging in Innovation: Evidence from the Spanish Innovation Survey." *Industry and Innovation* 21 (1): 1–19. doi:10.1080/13662716.2014.879252.

Eom, B., and K. Lee. 2010. "Determinants of Industry-Academy Linkages and Their Impact on Firm Performance: The Case of Korea as a Latecomer in Knowledge Industrialization." *Research Policy* 39: 625–639. doi:10.1016/j.respol.2010.01.015.

Fernandes, A., M. Côrtes, and M. Pinho. 2004. "Caracterização das pequenas e médias empresas de base tecnológica em São Paulo: Uma análise preliminar." *Economia e Sociedade* 13 (1): 151–173.

Fischer, B., S. Queiroz, and N. Vonortas. 2018. "On the Location of Knowledge-Intensive Entrepreneurship in Developing Countries: Lessons from São Paulo, Brazil." *Entrepreneurship & Regional Development* 30 (5–6): 612–638. doi:10.1080/08985626.2018.1438523.

Freeman, C., and L. Soete. 1997. *The Economics of Industrial Innovation*. 3rd ed. Cambridge: MIT Press.

Freitas, I., R. Marques, and E. Silva. 2013. "University-Industry Collaboration and Innovation in Emergent and Mature Industries in New Industrialized Countries." *Research Policy* 42: 443–453. doi:10.1016/j.respol.2012.06.006.

Galia, F., and D. Legros. 2004. "Complementarities between Obstacles to Innovation: Evidence from France." *Research Policy* 33: 1185–1199. doi:10.1016/j.respol.2004.06.004.

Gallouj, F., and M. Savona. 2009. "Innovation in Services: A Review of the Debate and a Research Agenda." *Journal of Evolutionary Economics* 19 (2): 149–172. doi:10.1007/s00191-008-0126-4.

Greene, W. 2011. *Econometric Analysis*. 7th ed. Boston: Pearson Education Publishing.

Hadjimanolis, A. 2003. "The Barriers Approach to Innovation." In *The International Handbook on Innovation*, edited by L. V. Shavinina, 559–573. Amsterdam: Elsevier.

Haeussler, C., H. Patzelt, and S. Zahra. 2012. "Strategic Alliances and Product Development in High Technology New Firms: The Moderating Effect of Technological Capabilities." *Journal of Business Venturing* 27 (2): 217–233. doi:10.1016/j.jbusvent.2010.10.002.

Hagedoorn, J. 2002. "Interfirm R&D Partnerships: An Overview of Major Trends and Patterns since 1960." *Research Policy* 31: 477–492. doi:10.1016/S0048-7333(01)00120-2.

Hagedoorn, J., A. Link, and N. Vonortas. 2000. "Research Partnerships." *Research Policy* 29: 567–586. doi:10.1016/S0048-7333(99)00090-6.

Hall, B. 2008. "The Financing of Innovation." In *Handbook of Technology and Innovation Management*, edited by S. Shane, 409–430. Hoboken: Wiley.

Hall, B., A. Link, and J. Scott. 2001. "Barriers Inhibiting Industry from Partnering with Universities: Evidence from the Advanced Technology Program." *The Journal of Technology Transfer* 26: 87–98. doi:10.1023/A:1007888312792.

Hoffman, K., M. Pajero, J. Bessant, and L. Perren. 1998. "Small Firms, R&D, Technology and Innovation in the UK: A Literature Review." *Technovation* 18: 39–55. doi:10.1016/S0166-4972(97)00102-8.

IBGE. 2016. *Pesquisa de Inovação 2014 - PINTEC 2014*. Rio de Janeiro: Instituto Brasileiro de Geografia e Estatística.

Kamien, M., and N. Schwartz. 1982. *Market Structure and Innovation*. Cambridge: Cambridge University Press.

Kanama, D., and K. Nishikawa. 2017. "What Type of Obstacles in Innovation Activities Make Firms Access University Knowledge? an Empirical Study of the Use of University Knowledge on Innovation Outcomes." *The Journal of Technology Transfer* 42 (4): 141–157. doi:10.1007/s10961-015-9459-y.

Katz, R., and T. Allen. 1982. "Investigating the Not-Invented-Here (NIH) Syndrome: A Look at the Performance, Tenure and Communication Pattern of 50 R&D Project Groups." *R&D Management* 12 (1): 7–19. doi:10.1111/j.1467-9310.1982.tb00478.x.

Kim, Y.-J., and N. Vonortas. 2014. "Cooperation in the Formative Years: Evidence from Small Enterprises in Europe." *European Management Journal* 32: 795–805. doi:10.1016/j.emj.2014.02.003.

Kruss, G., K. Lee, W. Suzigan, and E. Albuquerque. 2015. "Introduction." In *Developing National Systems of Innovation: University-Industry Interactions in the Global South*, edited by E. Albuquerque, W. Suzigan, G. Kruss and K. Lee, 1–27. Cheltenham: Edward Elgar.

Laursen, K., and A. Salter. 2004. "Searching High and Low: What Types of Firms Use Universities as a Source of Innovation?" *Research Policy* 33: 1201–1215. doi:10.1016/j.respol.2004.07.004.

Levinthal, D. 1996. "Learning and Schumpeterian Dynamics." In *Organization and Strategy in the Evolution of the Enterprise*, edited by G. Dosi and F. Malerba, 27–41. London: MacMillan.

López-Martínez, R., E. Medellín, A. Scanlon, and J. Solleiro. 1994. "Motivations and Obstacles to University Industry Cooperation (UIC): A Mexican Case." *R&D Management* 24 (1): 17–31. doi:10.1111/j.1467-9310.1994.tb00844.x.

Madrid-Guijarro, A., D. Garcia, and H. Van Auken. 2009. "Barriers to Innovation among Spanish Manufacturing SMEs." *Journal of Small Business Management* 47 (4): 465–488. doi:10.1111/jsbm.2009.47.issue-4.

Malerba, F., Y. Caloghirou, M. McKelvey, and S. Radosevic, eds. 2016. *Dynamics of Knowledge-Intensive Entrepreneurship: Business Strategy and Public Policy*. London and New York: Routledge.

March, J. 1991. "Exploration and Exploitation in Organizational Learning." *Organizational Science* 2 (1): 71–87. doi:10.1287/orsc.2.1.71.

Moraes, M., E. Lima, and A. Lobosco. 2011. "Competências para inovar em pequenas e médias empresas tecnológicas." *Revista de Administração e Inovação* 8 (4): 206–226.

Moraes Silva, D., and A. Furtado. 2017. "Modelos teóricos e interesses de mensuração no surgimento da pesquisa de inovação brasileira (Pintec)." *Revista Brasileira de Inovação* 16 (1): 97–128. doi:10.20396/rbi.v16i1.8649141.

Moraes Silva, D., A. Furtado, and N. Vonortas. 2018. "University-Industry R&D Cooperation in Brazil: A Sectoral Approach." *The Journal of Technology Transfer* 43 (2): 285–315. doi:10.1007/s10961-017-9566-z.

Mowery, D., and B. Sampat. 2005. "Universities in National Innovation Systems." In *The Oxford Handbook of Innovation*, edited by J. Fagerberg, D. C. Mowery, and R. Nelson, 209–239. Oxford: Oxford University Press.

Negassi, S. 2004. "R&D Co-Operation and Innovation: A Microeconometric Study on French Firms." *Research Policy* 33: 365–384. doi:10.1016/j.respol.2003.09.010.

Nelson, R. 1959. "The Simple Economics of Basic Scientific Research." *Journal of Political Economy* 67 (3): 297–306. doi:10.1086/258177.

OECD. 2005. *Oslo Manual: Guidelines for Collecting and Interpreting Innovation Data*. 3rd ed. Paris: Organization for Economic Co-operation and Development.

OECD. 2011. *ISIC REV. 3 TECHNOLOGY INTENSITY DEFINITION: Classification of Manufacturing Industries into Categories Based on R&D Intensities*. Paris: Organization for Economic Co-operation and Development.

Pellegrino, G., and M. Savona. 2017. "No Money, No Honey? Financial versus Knowledge and Demand Constraints on Innovation." *Research Policy* 46: 510–521. doi:10.1016/j.respol.2017.01.001.

Pinho, M., M. Côrtes, and A. Fernandes. 2002. "A fragilidade das empresas de base tecnológica em economias periféricas: Uma interpretação baseada na experiência brasileira." *Ensaios FEE* 23 (1): 135–162.

Pinto, H., M. Fernandez-Esquinas, and E. Uyarras. 2015. "Universities and Knowledge-Intensive Business Services (KIBS) as Sources of Knowledge for Innovative Firms in Peripheral Regions." *Regional Studies* 49 (11): 1873–1891. doi:10.1080/00343404.2013.857396.

Powell, W., and S. Grodal. 2005. "Networks of Innovators." In *The Oxford Handbook of Innovation*, edited by J. Fagerberg, D. C. Mowery, and R. Nelson, 56–85. Oxford: Oxford University Press.

Protogerou, A., Y. Caloghirou, and N. Vonortas. 2017. "Determinants of Young Firms' Innovative Performance: Empirical Evidence from Europe." *Research Policy* 46: 1312–1326. doi:10.1016/j.respol.2017.05.011.

Rothaermel, F., and D. Deeds. 2006. "Alliance Type, Alliance Experience and Alliance Management Capability in High-Technology Ventures." *Journal of Business Venturing* 21 (4): 429–460. doi:10.1016/j.jbusvent.2005.02.006.

Schumpeter, J. 1942. *Capitalism, Socialism and Democracy*. New York: Harper and Row.

Segarra-Blasco, A., J. Garcia-Quevedo, and M. Teruel-Carrizosa. 2008. “Barriers to Innovation and Public Policy in Catalonia.” *International Entrepreneurship and Management Journal* 4: 431–451. doi:10.1007/s11365-008-0086-z.

Shapira, P., J. Youtie, and L. Kay. 2011. “Building Capabilities for Innovation in SMEs: A Cross-Country Comparison of Technology Extension Policies and Programmes.” *International Journal of Innovation and Regional Development* 3 (3/4): 254–272. doi:10.1504/IJIRD.2011.040526.

Storey, D., and B. Tether. 1998. “Public Policy Measures to Support New Technology-Based Firms in the European Union.” *Research Policy* 26 (9): 1037–1057. doi:10.1016/S0048-7333(97)00058-9.

Tether, B. 2002. “Who Co-Operates for Innovation, and Why: An Empirical Analysis.” *Research Policy* 31: 947–967. doi:10.1016/S0048-7333(01)00172-X.

Tidd, J., J. Bessant, and K. Pavitt. 2005. *Managing Innovation: Integrating Technological, Market and Organizational Change*. 3rd ed. Hoboken: John Wiley and Sons.

Valentín, E. 2000. “University-Industry Cooperation: A Framework of Benefits and Obstacles.” *Industry & Higher Education* 14 (3): 165–172. doi:10.5367/000000000101295011.

Vanhaverbeke, W. 2006. “The Interorganizational Context of Open Innovation.” In *Open Innovation: Researching a New Paradigm*, edited by H. Chesbrough, W. Vanhaverbeke, and J. West, 205–219. Oxford: Oxford University Press.

Veugelers, R., and B. Cassiman. 1999. “Make and Buy in Innovation Strategies: Evidence from Belgian Manufacturing Firms.” *Research Policy* 28 (1): 63–80. doi:10.1016/S0048-7333(98)00106-1.

Vonortas, N. 1997. *Cooperation in Research and Development*. Dordrecht: Kluwer Academic Publishers.

Vonortas, N. 2009a. “Scale and Scope in Research.” In *European Science and Technology Policy*, edited by H. Dalanghe, U. Muldur, and L. Soete, 142–159. Cheltenham: Edward Elgar Publishing.

Vonortas, N. 2009b. “Innovation Networks in Industry.” In *Innovation Networks in Industries*, edited by F. Malerba and N. S. Vonortas, 27–44. Cheltenham: Edward Elgar Publishing.

Vonortas, N., and L. Zirulia. 2015. “Strategic Technology Alliances and Networks.” *Economics of Innovation and New Technology* 24 (5): 490–509. doi:10.1080/10438599.2014.988517.

# Appendix

**Table A1.** Contribution (%) to dimension *i*'s variance ($n$ = 3,736 firms).

| Obstacles | Dimension 1 | Dimension 2 |
|---|---|---|
| Excessive economic risk | **17.1** | **15.7** |
| High cost to innovate | **19.0** | **14.4** |
| Lack of adequate funding sources | **15.1** | 12.2 |
| Lack of qualified personnel | **12.3** | 10.2 |
| Lack of information on technology | 9.5 | **25.4** |
| Lack of information on markets | 9.3 | **13.0** |
| Organisational rigidities | 8.0 | 2.4 |
| Difficulty to comply with norms, standards and regulations | 9.7 | 2.8 |
| Innovation centralised in another company from the same group | 0.2 | 4.1 |
| Variance (%) | 89.5 | 0.9 |
| Cumulative variance (%) | 89.5 | 90.4 |

**Table A2.** Internal reliability coefficients (Cronbach's Alpha) for the composite independent variables (Aggregate Obstacles) ($n$ = 3,736 firms).

| Aggregate Obstacles | Specific Barriers | Cronbach's Alpha |
|---|---|---|
| Financial Obstacles | • Excessive economic risk<br>• High cost to innovate<br>• Lack of adequate funding sources | 0.9206 |
| Knowledge Obstacles | • Lack of qualified personnel<br>• Lack of information on technology<br>• Lack of information on markets | 0.8730 |
| Organisational Obstacles | • Organisational rigidities<br>• Innovation centralised in another company from the same corporate group<br>• Difficulty to comply with norms, standards and regulations | 0.5946 |

**Table A3.** Probit regression results with alternative independent variables (Full sample: $n$ = 3,736 firms).

| | Model 1 | | Model 2 | | Model 3 | | Model 4 | |
|---|---|---|---|---|---|---|---|---|
| Variables | Coefficients | Marginal effects | Coefficients | Marginal effects | Coefficients | Marginal effects | Coefficients | Marginal effects |
| FINOBS2 | | | 0.122*** | 0.011*** | | | 0.099*** | 0.009*** |
| | | | (0.033) | (0.003) | | | (0.035) | (0.003) |
| KNOBS2 | | | | | 0.175*** | 0.016*** | 0.120** | 0.011** |
| | | | | | (0.055) | (0.005) | (0.058) | (0.005) |
| GOV | 0.546*** | 0.053*** | 0.536*** | 0.051*** | 0.536*** | 0.051*** | 0.531*** | 0.051*** |
| | (0.083) | (0.008) | (0.084) | (0.008) | (0.083) | (0.008) | (0.084) | (0.008) |
| INNO | 0.358*** | 0.035*** | 0.351*** | 0.034*** | 0.356*** | 0.034*** | 0.352*** | 0.033*** |
| | (0.087) | (0.008) | (0.087) | (0.008) | (0.087) | (0.008) | (0.087) | (0.008) |
| HRD | 0.661*** | 0.064*** | 0.649*** | 0.062*** | 0.670*** | 0.064*** | 0.657*** | 0.063*** |
| | (0.088) | (0.008) | (0.088) | (0.008) | (0.088) | (0.008) | (0.088) | (0.008) |
| GRP | 0.200** | 0.019** | 0.232** | 0.022** | 0.212** | 0.020** | 0.235** | 0.022** |
| | (0.094) | (0.009) | (0.095) | (0.009) | (0.094) | (0.009) | (0.095) | (0.009) |
| IMP | 0.439*** | 0.042*** | 0.414*** | 0.040*** | 0.421*** | 0.040*** | 0.407*** | 0.039*** |
| | (0.083) | (0.008) | (0.083) | (0.008) | (0.083) | (0.008) | (0.083) | (0.008) |
| Sectoral dummies | YES | YES | YES | YES | YES | YES | YES | YES |
| Regional dummies | YES | YES | YES | YES | YES | YES | YES | YES |
| Constant | −1.947*** | | −2.041*** | | −1.961*** | | −2.034*** | |
| | (0.494) | | (0.499) | | (0.494) | | (0.243) | |
| Observations | 3,736 | 3,736 | 3,736 | 3,736 | 3,736 | 3,736 | 3,736 | 3,736 |
| Pseudo $R^2$ | 0.239 | | 0.247 | | 0.244 | | 0.249 | |

*** p<0.01. ** p<0.05. * p<0.1; Standard errors in parentheses

**Table A4.** Probit regression results with alternative independent variables (High-tech manufacturing: $n$ = 2,045 firms).

| | Model 5 | | Model 6 | | Model 7 | | Model 8 | |
|---|---|---|---|---|---|---|---|---|
| Variables | Coefficient | Marginal effects | Coefficient | Marginal effects | Coefficient | Marginal effects | Coefficient | Marginal effects |
| FINOBS2 | | | 0.110** | 0.010** | | | 0.095** | 0.009** |
| | | | (0.044) | (0.004) | | | (0.046) | (0.004) |
| KNOBS2 | | | | | 0.148* | 0.014* | 0.100 | 0.009 |
| | | | | | (0.079) | (0.007) | (0.082) | (0.008) |
| GOV | 0.569*** | 0.056*** | 0.569*** | 0.055*** | 0.571*** | 0.055*** | 0.571*** | 0.055*** |
| | (0.108) | (0.010) | (0.109) | (0.010) | (0.109) | (0.010) | (0.109) | (0.010) |
| INNO | 0.361*** | 0.035*** | 0.360*** | 0.035*** | 0.362*** | 0.035*** | 0.361*** | 0.035*** |
| | (0.113) | (0.011) | (0.114) | (0.011) | (0.114) | (0.011) | (0.114) | (0.011) |
| HRD | 0.777*** | 0.076*** | 0.767*** | 0.075*** | 0.784*** | 0.076*** | 0.773*** | 0.075*** |
| | (0.114) | (0.011) | (0.114) | (0.011) | (0.114) | (0.011) | (0.114) | (0.011) |
| GRP | 0.350*** | 0.034*** | 0.380*** | 0.037*** | 0.360*** | 0.035*** | 0.383*** | 0.037*** |
| | (0.124) | (0.012) | (0.125) | (0.012) | (0.124) | (0.012) | (0.125) | (0.012) |
| IMP | 0.475*** | 0.046*** | 0.445*** | 0.043*** | 0.453*** | 0.044*** | 0.435*** | 0.042*** |
| | (0.110) | (0.010) | (0.111) | (0.010) | (0.111) | (0.010) | (0.112) | (0.011) |
| Sectoral dummies | YES | YES | YES | YES | YES | YES | YES | YES |
| Regional dummies | YES | YES | YES | YES | YES | YES | YES | YES |
| Constant | −2.508*** | | −2.624*** | | −2.544*** | | −2.632*** | |
| | (0.407) | | (0.417) | | (0.407) | | (0.378) | |
| Observations | 2,045 | 2,045 | 2,045 | 2,045 | 2,045 | 2,045 | 2,045 | 2,045 |
| Pseudo $R^2$ | 0.300 | | 0.306 | | 0.303 | | 0.307 | |

*** p<0.01. ** p<0.05. * p<0.1; Standard errors in parentheses

**Table A5.** Probit regression results with alternative independent variables (KIBS: $n = 1,691$ firms).

| | Model 9 | | Model 10 | | Model 11 | | Model 12 | |
|---|---|---|---|---|---|---|---|---|
| Variables | Coefficients | Marginal effects | Coefficients | Marginal effects | Coefficients | Marginal effects | Coefficients | Marginal effects |
| FINOBS2 | | | 0.148*** | 0.013*** | | | 0.116** | 0.010** |
| | | | (0.051) | (0.004) | | | (0.055) | (0.005) |
| KNOBS2 | | | | | 0.214*** | 0.019*** | 0.145* | 0.013* |
| | | | | | (0.080) | (0.007) | (0.087) | (0.008) |
| GOV | 0.525*** | 0.049*** | 0.488*** | 0.044*** | 0.486*** | 0.044*** | 0.471*** | 0.043*** |
| | (0.135) | (0.012) | (0.136) | (0.012) | (0.136) | (0.012) | (0.136) | (0.012) |
| INNO | 0.371*** | 0.034*** | 0.349** | 0.032** | 0.365** | 0.033** | 0.349** | 0.032** |
| | (0.140) | (0.013) | (0.141) | (0.013) | (0.140) | (0.012) | (0.140) | (0.012) |
| HRD | 0.467*** | 0.043*** | 0.461*** | 0.042*** | 0.481*** | 0.044*** | 0.473*** | 0.043*** |
| | (0.144) | (0.013) | (0.144) | (0.013) | (0.144) | (0.013) | (0.144) | (0.013) |
| GRP | 0.025 | 0.002 | 0.061 | 0.005 | 0.035 | 0.003 | 0.060 | 0.005 |
| | (0.153) | (0.014) | (0.154) | (0.014) | (0.154) | (0.014) | (0.155) | (0.014) |
| IMP | 0.422*** | 0.039*** | 0.411*** | 0.037*** | 0.415*** | 0.038*** | 0.408*** | 0.037*** |
| | (0.132) | (0.012) | (0.132) | (0.012) | (0.131) | (0.012) | (0.132) | (0.012) |
| Sectoral dummies | YES | YES | YES | YES | YES | YES | YES | YES |
| Regional dummies | YES | YES | YES | YES | YES | YES | YES | YES |
| Constant | −1.227** | | −1.297** | | −1.211** | | −1.272** | |
| | (0.555) | | (0.318) | | (0.319) | | (0.320) | |
| Observations | 1,691 | 1,691 | 1,691 | 1,691 | 1,691 | 1,691 | 1,691 | 1,691 |
| Pseudo $R^2$ | 0.176 | | 0.188 | | 0.185 | | 0.191 | |

*** $p<0.01$. ** $p<0.05$. * $p<0.1$; Standard errors in parentheses.

# Harnessing adaptive capacity to close the pandora's box of open innovation

Maral Mahdad, Chiara Eleonora De Marco, Andrea Piccaluga and Alberto Di Minin

**ABSTRACT**

This paper focuses on how companies deploy structural properties of adaptive capacity (*multiplexity, redundancy* and *loose coupling*) to cope with the phenomenon of internal challenges of Open Innovation (OI) implementation, i.e. organisational and cultural changes. We developed a single case study, which offered significant findings. First, the multiplexity of relationships in OI settings helps to face the challenges of organisational and cultural changes by triggering trust formation and interaction. Second, redundancy has twofold elements: institutional logics redundancy triggers cultural change challenges which can be overcome through management practices and communications; task redundancy facilitates knowledge sharing and collaboration, thus helping to deal with organisational change challenges. Finally, loose coupling in OI settings facilitates social interconnectedness among members through management practices, helping to face organisational and cultural change challenges. We provide managerial and theoretical implication to deal with the challenges of OI in relation to both organisational and cultural changes.

## 1. Introduction

The paradigm of Open Innovation (OI) (Chesbrough 2003) gathered significant interest not only within the academic environment, but also in entrepreneurial settings. The academic research on OI has been developed until it became one of the most popular trends in the innovation management literature (Giannopoulou, Yström, and Ollila 2011; Oumlil and Juiz 2016). The scholarship on the topic of OI dedicated its attention to the benefits that the paradigm can offer to organisations that adopt an open approach to their innovation processes. Only more recently did scholars start focusing on the downsides embedded in its implementation, but the topic of the challenges arising from OI and how to face them efficiently remains underexplored.

Since the phenomenon of OI challenges received limited attention, there is no one literature stream that has been explaining it comprehensively. Furthermore, OI classifies as a multifaceted and complex phenomenon itself, whose understanding requires a combination of different theoretical perspectives into a broader framework (Vanhaverbeke and Cloodt 2014). Following this idea, we build on three different streams of the literature that, taken individually, would not exhaustively explain the phenomenon of OI challenges (Eisenhardt and Graebner 2007). In order to shed light on this topic, we limit our focus on the OI internal challenges of implementing organisational and cultural changes (De Marco et al. 2017) and analyse a specific mode of OI implementation: the university-industry collaboration (UIC). We respond to the call for research on the theme of which strategies companies apply in collaborating with academia in an OI scenario (Perkmann and Walsh 2007). In so doing, we build on the literature of adaptive capacity to shed light on the interactions among its structural properties of multiplexity, redundancy and loose-coupling, then exploring how these can be useful tools to apply in facing internal OI challenges in UIC.

Building on the streams of literature of Open Innovation, University-Industry Collaboration, and Adaptive Capacity, we aim at addressing the question of how an organisation deploys the structural properties of adaptive capacity to deal with the internal challenges of OI arising from its collaboration with universities. We based our analysis on 53 in-depth interviews with different stakeholders among eight laboratories joint between Telecom Italia (TIM) and five major Italian universities.

This article is organised into five sections. Following the Introduction, Section 2 presents the literatures on which we built the study, i.e. UIC, OI, and adaptive capacity. Section 3 includes the case study and methodology used in the empirical analysis. Section 4 analyzes and discusses the results obtained. Section 5 portrays the main implications, contributions and limitations of our research.

## 2. Theoretical background

### 2.1. University-industry collaboration

The topic of University-Industry Collaboration (UIC) has been widely explored from many angles and the literature on the topic is copious. The phenomenon is largely widespread due to the strong and many values that it provides to both industrial and academic partners: university considers industry to be a valuable partner in encouraging their research activities to expand into new contexts, ideas and research questions (D'Este and Perkmann 2011); on the other hand, industry regards universities as a stimulus for its internal innovation and a leverage for R&D expenditures (Salter and Martin 2001). Indeed, the increased availability and access to knowledge and highly skilled workers boosted the proliferation of actors participating in R&D activities and opened up the innovation process: large corporations lost the monopoly of knowledge and, hence, of R&D activities which are currently practised by multiple actors, ranging from start-ups and small businesses in general to universities and public research organisations (Chesbrough 2015). Collaboration with academia represents a source of improvement for firms' absorptive capacities and learning capabilities to be deployed for both exploration and exploitation activities (Bishop, D'Este, and Neely 2011). In this scenario, universities have become a major player with which to collaborate to develop leading-edge technologies accessing scientific breakthroughs and knowledge, empowering science, decreasing risks and costs of innovation, as well as using research laboratories and facilities (Bonaccorsi and Piccaluga 1994). In so doing, UIC and knowledge transfer result to be facilitated by the mediator of collaborative research centres, when the company and university carry out their collaboration with joint efforts (Lind, Styhre, and Aaboen 2013). In these contexts, the established laboratories are separate organisations, with rules and processes that differ from the pure industrial or academic ones, and in which industry employees and academics can work together on a daily basis (Thune and Gulbrandsen 2014).

The collaboration with the university has been included among the activities through which organisation can practice OI (Chesbrough 2006b; Lazzarotti and Manzini 2009; Rohrbeck, Hölzle, and Gemünden 2009). It is a specific mode of practising the inbound OI activity of searching for external knowledge, which includes 'buying R&D services from other organizations, such as universities, public research organizations, commercial engineers, or suppliers' (van de Vrande et al. 2009, 428). Despite the acknowledged advantages of UIC, OI scholars have been highlighting that the collaboration with academic partners implies particular difficulties related to the substantial divergence of cultural and organisational values (Ollila and Elmquist 2011; Lenz et al. 2016).

### *2.2. The challenges of implementing open innovation*

The OI approach has been adopted in the private sector by companies that wanted to branch out their boundaries and collaborate with partners in order to benefit from a wider range of technology, assets and knowledge, but also reduce the innovation costs and accelerate their time-to-market (Oumlil and Juiz 2016; Randhawa, Wilden, and Hohberger 2016). Scholars demonstrated the effectiveness argument for OI, showing that firms implementing OI strategies (OISs) can exploit diversified knowledge bases, integrate assets, and accelerate the innovation process offering better products and services on less uncertain market conditions (Almirall and Casadesus-Masanell 2010; Chesbrough 2003, 2006a; Chesbrough and Crowther 2006; Gassmann 2006; Gassmann and Enkel 2004; Huston and Sakkab 2006).

Despite literature extensively demonstrated the effectiveness of the OI paradigm, innovation itself remains a complex undertaking involving a variety of risks related to the impossibility of knowing *a priori* the outcome of the investments undertaken in R&D (Pisano 2015). This is even more so in an open process of innovation, since the actors, assets, interests, and loci involved are greater in number than in closed processes, in which the company conducts the R&D activity internally.

The OI is indeed a context-related phenomenon, presenting complexities and multidimensionality (Huizingh 2011) that give rise to obstacles to be faced in order to achieve the success of open strategies. The literature on the challenges of OI implementation is still scant and only recently have scholars highlighted the need to shed light on the issue of OI downsides (Dahlander and Gann 2010; Oumlil and Juiz 2016). De Marco et al. (2017) provided a first review of the literature on the challenges of implementing OI and proposed the two categories of challenges, internal and external, according to whether or not they arise inside or outside the organisation and, hence, the organisation is more or less able to deploy influential power over these challenges. For this study, we concentrated on the internal challenges of implementing OI and, particularly, we narrowed down the focus to the challenges of organisational and cultural changes.

The *organisational changes* implied in approaching OI are connected to the pervasiveness of the OIS, which cannot be limited to the units directly operating in R&D activities (Huston and Sakkab 2006), but that concerns the entire company as an 'organizational innovation' (Christensen 2006; Di Minin, Frattini, and Piccaluga 2010). Shifting towards an open approach in their innovation strategy, organisations need to adapt the setting of task distribution and responsibilities, and align these with the 'business as usual', reconfiguring the processes, resources and activities involved in the OIS. Despite OI having been recognised as a company-wide strategy (Huston and Sakkab 2006) and its implementation requiring wide organisational changes, the difficulties embedded in those changes have been left in the background of the studies conducted so far. The practical actions and processes undertaken by the companies that face the challenge differ depending on the characteristics of the single organisations embracing OI, thus remain a relatively underexplored issue.

The high-impact organisational changes related to OI even involve the adoption of *cultural changes*: a new approach to the entire company governance and innovation processes. The spread of an open culture within organisational boundaries appears as the main factor guaranteeing the sustainability of OI as a long-term strategy (Chesbrough and Crowther 2006; Dodgson, Gann, and Salter 2006; Di Minin, Frattini, and Piccaluga 2010). An open culture can foster proactivity and prompt collaboration (both within the organisation and outside of it), but it also provides the right motivations and vision to accept potential failures embedded in the implementation of such a pervasive new strategy like OI (Chiaroni, Chiesa, and Frattini 2010; Laursen and Salter 2006). Finally, communicating the new strategy in a straightforward and clear manner along with the higher levels of the organisation management fully committed endorsement are the premises for a successful OIS development (Huston and Sakkab 2006; Traitler, Watzke, and Sam Saguy 2011) as it secures the drivers necessary to face any internal resistance to the new approach. Indeed, one of the most common cultural challenges implied in OIS is known as the *Not-Invented-Here* (NIH) *syndrome*: R&D employees might distrust their external peers and not be willing to collaborate with them because they could undermine the relevance of their job offering better results and solutions (Chesbrough and Crowther 2006; Chiaroni, Chiesa, and Frattini 2010; Chesbrough and Brunswicker 2014; Kim, Kim, and Foss 2016; Lifshitz-Assaf 2017).

In the context of OI implemented in collaboration between academia and industry, the main difficulty is to align the interests of two organisations that highly differ in terms of values and goals (Lind, Styhre, and Aaboen 2013). Among the modes that industry has been trying to overcome the challenges of OI, particularly the ones concerning organisational and cultural changes, there is the attempt to tighten the interaction with academic partners as much as possible: close collaboration, in terms of both cognitive and geographical proximity (Boschma 2005; Wuyts et al. 2005; Bishop, D'Este, and Neely 2011), contributes to more effective collaboration. In the UIC literature, the establishment of cooperative research centres has been found to be a successful mode of practising collaboration and OI (Mahdad, Piccaluga, and Di Minin 2015). In these contexts, the two organisations can work together on a daily basis and find their way to cope with the challenges arising from the collaboration in an environment that totally differs from the traditional industrial or academic ones.

### 2.3. Adaptive capacity

The OI context of UIC is indeed a new setting, independent of the originating institutions, to which both organisations need to adapt deploying their efforts and specific actions in order to guarantee the sustainability of the collaboration and gain the benefits brought by OI. The general notion of adaptive capacity relates to systems' capabilities of enduring the challenges posed by discontinuities and disruptions, alleviating the impact of changes, or benefiting from new advantage opportunities overcoming uncertainty and instability to adapt into a new environment (Abbaszadeh and Boudaghi 2014; Fazey et al. 2007). Initially generated in the fields of engineering and sustainability management, the concept has then been applied in the literature of organisational strategy, as a tool to cope with innovation, cooperation and learning. In this context, the concept of adaptive capacity has been related to the dynamic capabilities literature, which specifically emphasises 'the firm's ability to integrate, build, and reconfigure internal and external competences to address rapidly changing environments' (Teece, Pisano, and Shuen 1997, 516). In their literature review on the dynamic capabilities, Wang and Ahmed (2007, 39) identify adaptive capabilities among the most important components of dynamic capabilities, and define them as the firm skills of aligning 'internal organizational factors with external environmental factors', timely and flexible. The scholars clearly distinguished them from the other components: innovative capabilities (i.e. coordinating the innovative behaviours and processes with strategic innovative orientation) and, particularly, absorptive capacities, identified following the definition of Cohen and Levinthal (1990), focusing on recognition, integration and commercialisation of valuable new external knowledge. While the relevance of innovative and absorptive capacity in the context of OI has been explored by the literature (Ahn et al. 2016; Zobel 2017), the role of adaptive capacities as defined by Wang and Ahmed (2007) has been neglected. Firms' adaptive capabilities consist of a strategic balance between the exploration and exploitation strategies allowed by applying resources and organisational structure flexibly, evolving along with the organisational needs (Staber and Sydow 2002; Sanchez 1995; Rindova and Kotha 2001). The core of adaptive capacity, hence, is the ability to find a proper balance between internal and external elements: firms need to be swift when adapting their internal organisational elements to the factors resulting from an evolving external environment (Wang and Ahmed 2007).

#### 2.3.1. The properties of adaptive capacity

Following Staber and Sydow (2002), we consider adaptive capacity as the firm's lasting proactivity in developing and applying new knowledge and timely reconfiguring in a changing environment. This organisational approach is dynamic and involves significant ambiguity and complexity from which management difficulties can arise. Management challenges and uncertain outcomes of the approach lie into the contradictions arising from the contrast embedded in the three structural properties that Staber and Sydow (2002) identified for adaptive capacity and that we adopt as a framework for this study: *multiplexity, redundancy* and *loose coupling.*

In their study, the scholars recall as the main characteristic of adaptive capacity the information-processing ability of a firm. Learning is essential and it usually appears as a '*double loop*' approach characterised by a higher level of organisational reflexivity meant as more relevant for complex and tacit knowledge and, in situations of uncertainty, implying recursive interplays between the organisation and the environment. With the organisation being proactive in its environment, not only does it keep up with the changes, but it is also able to anticipate them, because of the firm's projection towards the future. An organisation with adaptive capacities has a learning process that is faster than the pace of changes, and therefore, it is able to evolve its organisational routines.

Using Giddens' structuration theory (1984) and the recursive interaction between the two dimensions of structure and interaction, Staber and Sydow (2002) build the structural properties of adaptive capacity: *multiplexity, redundancy and loose coupling.*

*Multiplexity* consists of the availability of different typologies of knowledge exchanges through different linkages. It can lead to an increased diversification and spread of knowledge, but also a higher access to knowledge. This is only relevant for adaptive capabilities when knowledge exchanges assume significance directly depending on the rules enforced in the organisation and interpretation schemes of the actors involved in the exchange. Multiplexity is relevant for adaptive capacity whether the interpretation of knowledge flows is consistent and pacific, potential abuses of powers are avoided in order to guarantee the openness in creating and sharing knowledge, and the management of the firms has a proper control of multiplexity.

*Redundancy* is often considered as a waste of resources, including excess of employees, extra productive yet unoccupied capacity, overlapping jurisdictions, tolerance of mistakes, broad jobs descriptions, duplication of communication channels, etc. The organisational attitude is usually to limit redundancy to pursue efficiency, but redundancy also presents some positive elements. It can enhance adaptive capacity when relating to information, tasks and relations. Redundant information, combined with multiplex knowledge structures, can guarantee the proper transmission of information. Task redundancy results from the duplication of functions in the organisation, which can guarantee that, in case of failure of one element, the organisation will not fail since there will be another active element pursuing the same function of the failed one. Redundancy of relation refers to the linkages among actors of knowledge in several ways. Again, the failure of a relationship can be easily solved by replacing it with a similar one. These elements of redundancy can make the organisation more prone to accept failures and mistakes, hence more prone to take on risks and innovate. This notwithstanding, redundancy could also hamper adaptive capacities because it can lead to increased competition and limit the variability whether the communication gains the saturation levels, becoming just repetitive.

*Loose Coupling* emerges when a system presents few or weak common variables among its elements. In the adaptive capacity, loose coupling consists of the decentralisation of control, slow and unequal flows of knowledge and information. The interpretation criteria adopted in the organisation might be varied and inconsistent, and evaluation of the firm's rules is extremely fragmented. In loose coupling, the demand for a proper management is high, but it is usually inadequate and can jeopardise the same survival of the system. On the one hand, the loose coupling can increase survival chance when possibilities coming from new knowledge are unclear, and this property can secure that some other organisational elements would provide a better understanding of the environment. When the coupling is tight, it can have the opposite effect and make the achievement of a stable state difficult, because any disturbance can have an impact on the system. Furthermore, when the tie is too tight, it might jeopardise an organization's survival in case of uncertainty in the environment, because the strategy of the firm became too coherent. On the other hand, loose coupling connection of individuals can enhance adaptive capacity because individuals can have multiple connections with other parts of the system; therefore, they are able to enhance the network and provide a wider range of information source.

The analysis of adaptive capacity outcomes has been neglected until now, especially considering the relations existing among its structural properties, institutionalisation and structuration processes. Concerning structural properties, probably the three that we consider following extant literature (Staber and Sydow 2002) are not the only possible ones contributing to the emergence of adaptive capacity. Indeed, especially in inter-organisational networks, 'trust' can be considered as an essential facilitator of the organisational change and innovation, even though the factors that connect trust with the other properties are still not clear.

Our work applies the structural properties of adaptive capacity to analyse the phenomenon of OI challenges in the context of university-industry collaboration. This study answers the question of how the company deploys its adaptive capacities to cope with internal OI challenges.

## 3. Methodology

### *3.1. Research setting and case selection*

Our study is based on a single case study of the largest telecommunication company in Italy, the Telecom Italia Group (TIM), a joint-stock company providing services and infrastructures that go beyond the Italian borders.

Innovation has been at the root of TIM for a long time and it dates back to the nineties, when the first radical change occurred: the privatisation of Telecom Italia group. In 2001, the main innovative activities of TIM were centralised in their spin-off company, TILab (Cesaroni, Di Minin, and Piccaluga 2004), pursuing technological collaboration strategies with different partners, and conducting activities ranging from R&D (e.g. scouting, testing, performance evaluation, technology trials), to the development of EU funded projects, collaboration with vendors and academia (Source: TILab report). Nonetheless, innovative activities of TIM did not remain limited to TILab, especially after the emergence of the OI phenomenon, when the company started investing on collaboration with external sources of knowledge producers, like universities. In 2012, TIM launched the Joint Open Labs (JOLs) project for the scouting of external innovative ideas, to anticipate the diffusion of the OI model across the main university campuses in Italy.

Since 2012, eight JOLs were established among five major Italian universities to bring possible innovative proficiencies within the same centre. The classic model of innovation adopted by TIM changed to an agile model of innovation, which enhances co-creation and co-development. The Agile OI framework of TIM takes a step forward to get closer to adopt the OI paradigm and collaboration and, since their establishments, JOLs achieved major success in the development of their R&D activities (see Table1).

According to TIM's management, Joint Open Labs play a key role in the competitive innovation environment. This particular model of collaboration encourages inter-organisational relationships and interactions between academia and the industry. Co-location is also an important factor:

**Table 1.** TIM JOLs achievements.

| | |
|---|---|
| People | >50 young people hired by TIM after participating in JOL's activities |
| | >60 PhD students |
| | >30 interns |
| Financial Resources | >€ 960K invested in research projects |
| | > € 450K invested in materials |
| | € 200K invested in structures |
| Innovative ideas | >10 innovative ideas turned into fully formed business proposals and commercial opportunities for Telecom Italia |
| Intellectual Property | 27 patents filed |
| | 4 MPEG-standard patents filed |
| | 1 Spin-Up-eligible patent |
| Collaboration | 30+ foreign top-ranking academic institutions |
| | 15 |
| Diversity | 15 different nationalities present at the JOLs |
| Research output | >250 research papers |
| | 40 training seminar |
| | >30 JOL blog articles |
| Dissemination | >20 events |
| | 2 Big Data Challenges |
| | >1,100 individuals involved |
| | >650 international teams |
| | >40 university teams |

> [A]n open space for open minds, in which researchers from different fields come together to combine their diverse skills (both internal and external to the company) acquire know-how, develop new business strategies and open up new avenues for financial growth. (Source: Company Report)

These eight JOLs are located within five major Italian universities and in different cities: Politecnico di Torino, Politecnico di Milano, Università degli Studi di Trento with the Fondazione Bruno Kessler, Scuola Superiore Sant'Anna (Pisa), Università degli Studi di Catania (Figure 1).

Before confirming TIM as the final case for this study, pilot interviews were used to identify whether TIM had the potential of answering the research question. Furthermore, the selection process was based on three requirements that the case needed to meet: 1) whether the company implements and adopts OI strategies across units and extensively, 2) diagnosing existing challenges identified from literature through field observations and pilot interviews, and 3) signs of engagement and commitment in facing the challenges, putting effort to actively react to their arising. Pilot interviews and observations were mostly focused on day-to-day activities of individuals and specific situations. After this, it was possible to confirm that the selected case met all the three criteria posed in the conditions for selection.

### 3.2. *Methodological approach*

Our study aims at developing new insights into the process of how the company deploys its adaptive capacities to cope with internal OI challenges. Since the focus of our research is not solely on exploring existing stories (inductive) but rather to comprehend and explain the influence of existing processes in overcoming challenges of OI implementation (deductive) the grounded theory approach was our starting point. The grounded theory approach appears suitable in our case because of its systematic and structured analysis of the data (Charmaz 2011). Furthermore, as the study was not completely empirically driven from the

**Figure 1.** JOLs' location.

data generated by participants, but also taking into account existing theories and literature, the *Multi-Grounded Theory (MGT)* approach was chosen accordingly. In the MGT approach, certain aspects of inductivism and deductivism are combined (Goldkuhl and Cronholm 2010). Using this methodological approach within our setting the theory is grounded in: a) empirical data, data from interviews in our case study; b) pre-existing theories selected to explain the phenomenon, in our case the adaptive capacity one; and c) compliance within the theory itself, a relationship between elements of the theory. We then used four stages of analysis in the MGT approach to generate theories: 1) inductive coding, 2) conceptual refinement, 3) pattern coding and 4) theory condensation (Goldkuhl and Cronholm 2010). The details concerning data and analysis are presented in the following paragraphs.

### *3.3. Data collection*

In order to answer the question of how the company deploys its adaptive capacities to cope with internal OI challenges, we chose a single-case study approach. This approach was selected according to the need of gathering in-depth data, rich with information on the phenomenon (Yin 2008). As Eisenhardt (1989) indicated, the qualitative approach is useful for understanding the rationale or theory underlying relationships.

Our research relies relied on theoretical sampling: the selected case was chosen for theoretical, not statistical, reasons. This research was carried out in Italy between 2014 and 2015.

To address the research question and contribute to the phenomenon of OI challenges and adaptive capacity theory, we conducted 53 interviews within eight joint laboratories of Telecom Italia (see Table 2).

**Table 2.** TIM JOLs dimensions and interviewees profiles.

| TIM JOLs | Lab 1 | Lab 2 | Lab 3 | Lab 4 | Lab 5 | Lab 6 | Lab 7 | Lab 8 |
|---|---|---|---|---|---|---|---|---|
| Size* | 20–25 | 20 | 15–20 | 15–20 | 20 | 10–15 | 10–15 | 20 |
| **Informants** | | | | | | | | |
| Lab director | 1 | 1 | 1 | 1 | 1 | 1 | 1 | 1 |
| TIM employees | 7 | 6 | 3 | 2 | 2 | 2 | 2 | 5 |
| PhD students | 1 | 3 | 2 | 2 | 2 | 3 | 0 | 3 |

* Size refers to the number of company employees and academic people participating in the activity of the JOL.

The main data collection method was to conduct semi-structured interviews using an open-ended interview protocol. The semi-structured interviews allowed the interviewees to express their comments freely; therefore, in-depth data and insights were collected. In total, we performed 53 interviews with different representatives from university and industry such as company employees, lab directors, and PhD students that are involved in the OI implementation of TIM. In designing the interview questions, we focused on a selected set of dimensions extracted from the literature. However, as is common in case study research, new dimensions started to reveal themselves in the course of the interviews. In our face-to-face interviews, we asked interviewees to describe the process they go through on a day-to-day basis. In particular, we asked them to describe daily interactions with different actors and their engagement level, and then to explain how proximity influenced their routine job, interaction, and communication.

### 3.4. Data analysis

The qualitative data were analyzed using the coding process described by Goldkuhl and Cronholm (2010) in the multi-grounded theory approach. Goldkuhl and Cronholm (2010) noted that open coding and non-predefined assumptions are the main assets for this approach. But, considering the pre-existing theories and grounding them as well, one finds a deductive process in addition to the inductive one. We started our analysis by diving deep into each interview and writing extended case reports for each of them. In the analysis process, we transcribed interview data and combined them with the questionnaire and archival data, including published and unpublished reports, to then conduct a triangulation of data sources for each interview, followed by the codification of the interview transcripts. Figure 2 represents the coding scheme of our study.

First, we started the open and inductive coding with the least predefined concepts and categories generated by data. The guiding questions were used during the open coding process to help identify emerging concepts related to the research questions such as: how is this particular OI approach (UIC) practised in the day to day life of participants? What is the role of partners in this setting? Are there any issues mentioned by the interviewees with regard to the collaboration? How do interviewees perceive addressing those issues/challenges? Subsequently, relevant lines in the data answering the above questions were highlighted. A second researcher went through the coding process to avoid any pre-assumptions and match interpretations.

Second, we conceptually refined the categories in an analytical way. That includes using field notes and observations that backed up our data. For each concept and category developed during open coding process, we included context, location and the language determination. For example, any category was then conceptually refined with

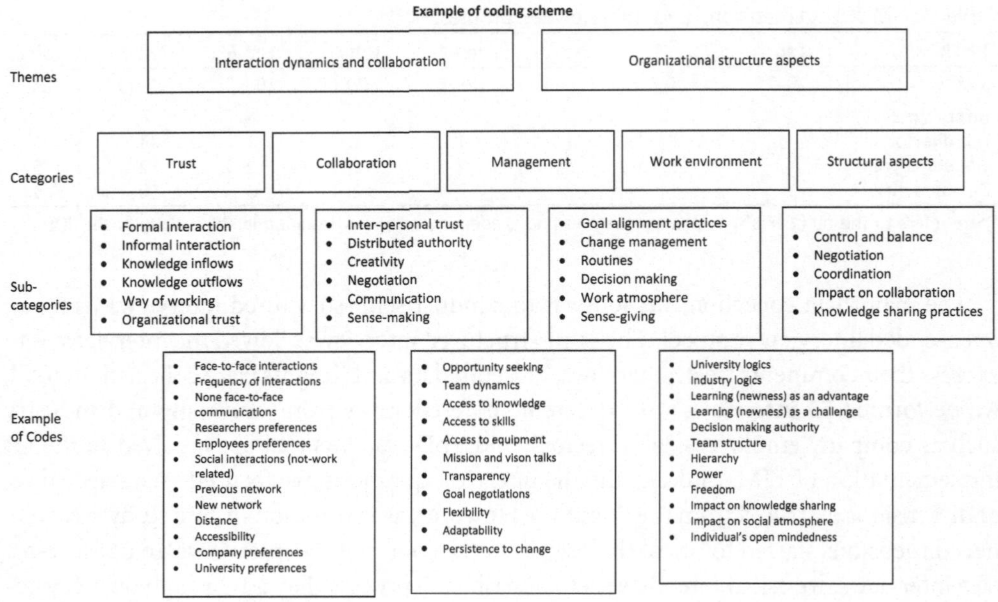


**Figure 2.** Coding scheme.

regard to where it was taking place, the context that explains this particular phenomenon and whether quality, process, attribute etc. are involved.

Third, the labels and concepts developed in the inductive coding were put in categories and sub-categories. In this coding process pattern, we found relationships among categories and sub-categories that explain the conditions and results of the actions. These patterns were then illustrated in graphical forms and the final clean version is summarised in Figure 3.

Last, we ground the existing theory – in our case Adaptive Capacity – with the three stages of validity to complete the theory grounding process. We first tested if the theory emerged was in line with the data, second if it was in accordance with existing theories, and finally if the existing theories help to structure the analysis process. In this phase of the analysis, we built on the deductivism approach by using the theory to ground the theory. This helped us to achieve a more clear and cohesive theory.

## 4. How adaptive capacities' properties impact OI challenges

Building on the theory of adaptive capacity and its properties, we explored how the *Multiplexity, Redundancy*, and *Loose Coupling* properties can impact the challenges of OI. We found that differences in mechanisms that occur when implementing OISs could be explained through the structural properties of adaptive capacity (Figure 3). Our analyses showed that each of the adaptive capacity properties can generate a positive impact on the organisational and cultural challenges raised by OIS. With the only exception of the duality triggered by the Redundancy of institutional logics, the practices characterising the properties result helpful in handling the difficulties related to the collaboration, limiting the impact of the challenges on the outcome of the innovation activities, as described in the following paragraph.

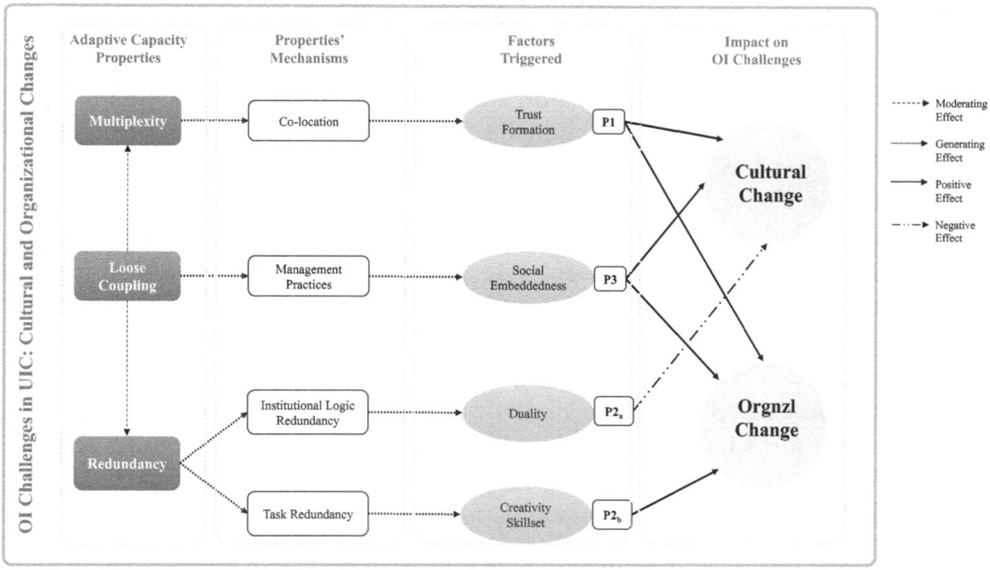


**Figure 3.** The lens of adaptive capacity properties over the internal challenges of OI.

### *4.1. Multiplexity as a trigger of trust formation and interactions*

Co-locating Telecom Italia and the Universities in the JOLs was a strategic decision of the company to set up a collaborative environment and develop knowledge spill-overs for the members, i.e. individuals working in the industry on the one hand and the university on the other.

> *I like this type of setting because it somehow changed the traditional approach of working with professors: they are only hundred meters away and discussing some issues in person is much easier for both parties.* (Internal TIM employee)

Within the JOLs, different types of knowledge were flowing in simultaneously from different sources (industry and university) and exchanged through a variety of diversified communication channels, both formal and informal. In this scenario, multiplexity resulted in the availability of multiple channels of communication and approaches to an interaction that favours the creation of a trustful social setting. These multiplexity mechanisms triggered the formation of trust among the members of the JOLs, which allowed to easily discuss and smoothen cultural frictions. In our case, the emergent trust is a direct result of the structure and formation of dyads and ties within these laboratories. This is driven not only from the breadth of relationships formed, but also the depth of the multiplexity of relationships. The type of relationships member developed within this setting varies between laboratories. In the laboratories where multiple types of formal and informal relationships coexist at the same time, we observe a faster pace of dealing with cultural change challenges of OI.

> *I'm able to get hold of the researchers quickly and it is awesome to have a round table without any logistic problem. So we are here and every time we can set up our meeting with*

> *other partners very easily. They can easily come here or we can go there and maybe this is a big advantage* (Internal TIM employee)

Furthermore, multiplexity of relationships can be translated into a variety of interactions that members develop. As a multiplex relationship results in enhanced commitment and the need for coping with different partners' preferences, it supports the development of higher levels of trust (Lee et al. 2010). As we see in our case, the existence of multiplex relationships triggered higher trust formation, resulting in a less conflictual collaboration. Members of an organisation shape the organisation itself. As a result of multiplexity of relationships among members, which leads to interpersonal trust formation, organisational trust at the collective level between the university and industry emerged. The occurrence of organisational multiplexity offered to the players co-located within the JOLs setting multiple and diversified interactive practices and processes, both formal and informal, that help dealing with the burdens of organisational changes related to the OI collaboration.

Based on these findings, we propose the following:

***Proposition 1:*** *Multiplexity of communication channels and organizational relationships within OI settings helps to face the cultural and organizational change challenges of OI by triggering trust formation and interactions.*

### *4.2. Redundancy as a double-edged sword*

Our interviewees reported difficulties in identifying their reference person. The situation was more evident for Ph.D. students, as they claimed to be committed to both academic and industrial sides. However, the issue concerned also company representatives, reporting to be dealing with an *ambiguous* situation. We found management practices to be useful in gaining benefits from redundancy, enabling the right channels for interaction between members and influencing how the ties and interactions are shaped, therefore positively impacting the challenge of cultural changes in the OI setting.

> *If it is just a strictly scientific issue, of course I would just inform my tutor at the university but when it is a more practical issue, I contact somebody from Telecom.* (PhD student)

> *Compared with universities, we have quite different points of view, but it is very interesting to create the link in our day-to-day job.* (Internal TIM employee)

We also observed that the issue of institutional duality inhibited collaborating closely with the other party. We found that the dual commitment of the actors implies the creation of dual institutional logics that might not be difficult to sustain, but certainly requires the right mix of strategy to overcome the ambiguity. We found management practices to be useful in order to benefit from redundancy in an efficient way, enabling the right channels for the interaction between members, which also relates to the multiplexity of relationships as it is driven from the ties and interactions among actors.

Nonetheless, we also found that, in some cases, interviewees were interpreting acting in a multi-culture environment useful for innovative activities and creativity. Employees in this setting faced a new set of tasks that mismatched the tasks of 'where they come from'. This new path helped individuals in developing individual mechanisms to deal with unknown situations or collaborative partners. Employees working with Ph.D. students had to deploy new sets of skills in order to carry on collaboration on a constructive basis. Many informants reported that being away from their usual routines in the company and involved in the routine characterising the activity of the academic partner activity stimulated them to be more creative and increased their learning ability to adapt to the new organisation of the work.

> *After seven years, my job was becoming a repetitive routine in the company and the type of work was flat and uninteresting. This project took place at the right time when I was just working with the project manager to contribute to the idea of open labs.* (TIM laboratory manager)

Despite task redundancy resulted to be beneficial for the collaborative setting, redundancy in identity generated a duality that triggered cultural challenges that employees faced in adapting to a new environment. In this context, trust between members from university and industry facilitated the process of negotiation for building a shared logic. The process of fostering trust within organisations is a result of effective communication orchestrated through management practices implemented by laboratory directors. According to our empirical setting, labs with effective communication techniques speed up the benefits reaped from task redundancy more than the ones lacking direction. Therefore, we propose the following:

***Proposition 2a:*** *Redundancy of institutional logics within OI settings generates duality dynamics in the members of the collaboration, triggering cultural challenges of OI implementation.*

***Proposition 2b:*** *Task redundancy within OI settings triggers creativity demanding individuals to act on multiple various tasks, enhancing their skill sets and lubricating collaboration, thus helping in facing organizational change challenge of OI.*

### 4.3. Loose coupling through management practices

The role of managers in identifying legitimacy and norms in organisations is undeniable. In joint university-industry laboratories, where actors might easily face divergence, leaders are the ones responsible for establishing coherent rules and norms. However, how can an organisation with no hierarchy and different levels and typologies of scientific background sustain divergent rules and redundancy?

> *The intangible asset that we have, which I think is probably the most important as a person, is freedom. As a Lab director, I felt that I had enough space to move about . So, I could really be a sort of entrepreneur within the company and I could even make some mistakes so I really have the freedom to have a go and bring some proposals to the table, ready to go in directions that nobody previously had thought.* (TIM laboratory manager)

> *It is amazing because they (the professors) are really approachable and even they use "TU" instead of "LEI", which is less formal.* (Internal TIM employee)

Our data show that JOLs that practice loose coupling between the hierarchical levels of the unit manage to sustain organisational and cultural changes of adopting OIS. This was driven from creating a socially embedded atmosphere where members would not face a strong hierarchy in their routines.

> *My experience says it works. It works when you understand this cultural difference; then you can deal with the academia to give them what they need and vice versa.* (Internal TIM employee)

Loose coupling consists of a range of actions that goes from addressing a problem, to organising meetings and encouraging frequent interactions. In the laboratories where individuals were given responsibilities, and power was distributed among members, we observed a healthier environment which led to withstanding the challenges of OI implementation. Yet laboratory directors played a significant role in giving a sense of the activities internally. Having said that, we also observed that in an environment with too high loose coupling levels, i.e. with fewer management practices being implemented, members faced challenges in identifying the laboratory goals.

> *[The company] left me a lot of room to explore my ideas, I took the project where it should go and I didn't feel much constraint. But at some point they wanted to make a product out of this research. There was no pressure for it; they know that this is a long-term research so the final goal of having something saleable maybe is far away from this short period.* (Ph.D. student)

Proper management mechanisms are found to be essential for the success of OI network through enabling the right channels for members' interaction, which has a moderating influence on the negative impact of cultural changes challenges. In this context, directors elaborate on practices that enable the lab understanding its own divergent and mixed-cultural environment through communicating the organisational goals to the members. In such hybrid environments, tight coupling by any of the actors involved might result in mistrust and prevent free knowledge sharing. On the contrary, loose coupling is useful for organisations in which members hardly define the culture and organisational structure in which they operate.

Power and control influence how social interactions are shaped within organisations and these interactions play a crucial role in a knowledge-intensive setting where members need to be socially interconnected to transfer knowledge successfully (Roberts 2000).

Given the loosely coupled environment, collaborative and accredited directors facilitate dynamics of knowledge sharing in such workplace. In our case, we discovered that different management approaches, namely loosely coupled or tightly coupled and OIS outcome, go hand in hand. Within teams of individuals with different abilities and ambitions, when members take responsibility of their team and coordinate it unofficially, such behaviours enhance the effectiveness of collaboration in problem-solving processes. This might be due to the co-existence of highly skilled professionals in one single OI team that communicate and share knowledge efficiently leveraging on diversified skills and learning tools. To conclude, our final proposition is:

***Proposition 3:*** *Loose coupling within OI settings facilitates social interconnectedness among members through management practices that helping individuals to deal with organizational and cultural change challenges of OI. These practices also involve the orchestration of multiplex communication challenges that, dealing with the factors triggered by task redundancy, moderate the negative impact of duality on the challenges of implementing cultural changes.*

## 5. Discussion and conclusion

This research addressed the under-explored area of how an organisation deals with OI internal challenges arising in the context of UIC within joint laboratories – which are one specific mode of implementing inbound OI. Our study aimed at answering the research question of how the company deploys its adaptive capacities to manage internal OI challenges arising in the collaboration with the university. Building on the theory of adaptive capacity, we found that, to deal with challenges of OIS implementation, the company leverages its internal capacities and organisational structure.

First, we found that multiplexity of relationships within an OI setting helps to minimise the negative impact of the challenge of implementing cultural and organisational changes by triggering trust formation and organisational interactions. High levels of trust emerged within teams composed by internal TIM employees and Ph. D. students due to the availability of multiple, frequent and diversified channels of communication and interactions. In the co-location setting of the JOLs, multiplexity resulted in social embeddedness within a network of individuals and, hence, higher effectiveness of knowledge transfer activities. Our case showed how the proper management of a combination of formal and informal diversified channels of interactions among members coming from different types of institutions (i.e. university and industry) working together under the same roof eases the emergence of spill-overs and, thus of knowledge transfer. In this OI setting, knowledge can flow through concurrent and even unconscious channels, i.e. the concept of *knowledge leak* as defined by Alberti and Pizzurno (2017). Exploring knowledge multiplexity in the context of start-ups involved in OI networks, these scholars highlighted that the multiplexity of relationships and interactions channels among members of OI setting fosters the simultaneous exchange of different knowledge types (in our case academic and industrial) that are simultaneous and non-excludable (Alberti and Pizzurno 2017). Our result is in line with previous studies and confirms the essential nature of relationship multiplexity in shaping the genesis and functioning of collaboration networks (Maggioni, Breschi, and Panzarasa 2013).

Second, we identified two types of redundancy, namely *institutional logics* and *task redundancy*. Redundancies within our context have different influences on the challenges of OI implementation. On one side, redundancy of institutional logics results in having a negative impact because it triggers cultural change challenges, which can be moderated through an efficient management of multiple and diverse communication channels. Laboratory directors are required to deploy mixed management strategies to foster trust and shared logics among OI network members. On the other hand, task redundancy helps the organisation to deal with the cultural change challenges of OI implementation and facilitates knowledge sharing and collaboration. Members of an organisation, when involved in a new organisational structure, tend to learn new skills and be more flexible. These individuals manage to collaborate with partners that apply different logics by coming out of their routine skill 'boxes', trying out new routines and tasks and being creative, which ease the implementation of organisational changes. Our results confirm previous literature highlighting that OISs in organisations can benefit from redundancy when it leads to enhanced and diversified individuals skills (Hafkesbrink and Schroll 2010).

However, future research should unravel the issues related to the application of the redundancy property of adaptive capacity in its potentials applications to answer the question of how management practices could be beneficial in balancing redundancy in open and collaborative environments. Indeed, despite previous research suggested that minimising redundancy between partners is an essential aspect for constructing an effective collaborative network (Burt 1992), in this study, we observed both the negative and the positive impact of redundant information within the OI setting.

Third, we contributed to the research on the effect of loose coupling on the innovation network (Dhanaraj and Parkhe 2006). In line with previous studies, we argue that in order to deal with both the challenges of organisational and cultural change in OI implementation, managers should avoid too strong a focus on hierarchical authorities favouring the design of loosely coupled environments. This is mainly relevant for knowledge-intensive settings, in which members are highly skilled and ambitious professionals (Pichault 1995). We argue that loose coupling within OI settings facilitates social embeddedness among members thus helping individuals to deal with organisational and cultural change challenges of OI.

Finally, our findings offer a relevant contribution to the theory of adaptive capacity. With this study, we aimed at interconnecting the properties of adaptive capacity of organisations in addition to introducing the discourse of OI as an empirical setting into this framework. Organisations can indeed benefit from multiplexity and redundancy through management practices of loose coupling. We showed that a loosely coupled system can be beneficial for an open and collaborative network through the implementation of appropriate management practices. First, loose coupled management practices generate social embeddedness that eases the implementation of both organisational and cultural changes; second, those practices can orchestrate multiplex communication channels and interactions that foster the creation of trust among the members of the system. Third, this orchestration of the mechanisms of multiplexity moderates the negative impact of duality dynamics on cultural changes challenges triggered the redundancy of institutional logics. These findings show how the loose coupling can play a balancing role among the structural properties of the adaptive capacity of organisations operating in an OI setting.

In addition, a further significant conclusion of this study involves the inter-relation of OI challenges of implementing cultural and organisational change: minimising the negative impact of one of them can influence and trigger positive effect on the other due to the emergence of social embeddedness through management practices especially in this particular way of collaboration. Therefore, we also contributed shedding light on the phenomenon of OI challenges by discovering how TIM handled the internal challenges of OI implementation through the execution of adaptive capacity practices.

Our study is not free of limitations, which can be addressed in future research. Firstly, our qualitative study aimed at applying the theory of adaptive capacity in the context of challenges of OI implementation, but further qualitative studies on a similar context are needed to strengthen our findings. In addition, this research explored the innovative perspective of applying the theoretical lens of adaptive capacity and its structural properties to the phenomenon of the OI internal challenges arising in a UIC setting. The scenario of the extant literature on OI has been offering several valuable contributions based on the application of other theoretical approaches to the OI phenomenon (e.g. dynamic capabilities, dynamic capacity, assimilation capacity, absorptive capacity). To the best of our knowledge, this is the first study applying the theoretical concepts of adaptive capacity to the research on OI. Nonetheless, we want to point out that other theoretical perspectives should be tested in this context, in order to explore the under-researched field of the challenges of OI, but also to empirically test other organisational capacities and alternative properties of the adaptive capacities that could be applied in dealing with OI challenges. Only then, large-scale studies could be utilised to facilitate the generalizability of these research results. Finally, a longitudinal case study approach could be applied in order to further enhance our understanding of how a firm actually faces challenges of OI implementation over time.

Our study offers implications not only for industrial managers and scholars, but also for university actors. Communication efforts are needed to ease the collaboration among actors with different mind-sets and objectives. An effective collaboration requires alignment of interests and matching of different organisational cultures, leveraging on redundancy and multiplexity. For these reasons, special endeavours in training and education by experts and/or facilitators could be a prerequisite of less-conflictive OI settings especially when partners differ for institutional logics and organisational culture.

## Disclosure statement

No potential conflict of interest was reported by the authors.

## ORCID

Maral Mahdad http://orcid.org/0000-0001-6612-5664

## References

Abbaszadeh, M., and A. Boudaghi. 2014. "The Effect of Ethical Leadership on Organizational Adaptive Capacity (The Case Study: Employees of Tabriz University)." *Journal of Public Administration* 6 (2): 298–308.

Ahn, J. M., Y. Ju, T. H. Moon, T. Minshall, D. Probert, S. Y. Sohn, and L. Mortara. 2016. "Beyond Absorptive Capacity in Open Innovation Process: The Relationships between Openness, Capacities and Firm Performance." *Technology Analysis and Strategic Management* 28 (9): 1009–1028. doi:10.1080/09537325.2016.1181737.

Alberti, F. G., and E. Pizzurno. 2017. "Oops, I Did It Again! Knowledge Leaks in Open Innovation Networks with Start-Ups." *European Journal of Innovation Management* 20. doi:10.1108/EJIM-11-2015–0116.

Almirall, E., and R. Casadesus-Masanell. 2010. "Open versus Closed Innovation: A Model of Discovery and Divergence." *Academy of Management Review* 35 (1): 27–47.

Bishop, K., P. D'Este, and A. Neely. 2011. "Gaining from Interactions with Universities: Multiple Methods for Nurturing Absorptive Capacity." *Research Policy* 40 (1): 30–40. doi:10.1016/j.respol.2010.09.009.

Bonaccorsi, A., and A. Piccaluga. 1994. "A Theoretical Framework for the Evaluation of University-Industry Relationships." *R&D Management* 24 (3): 229–247. doi:10.1111/j.1467-9310.1994.tb00876.x.

Boschma, R. 2005. "Proximity and Innovation: A Critical Assessment." *Regional Studies* 39 (1): 61–74. doi:10.1080/0034340052000320887.

Burt, R. S. 1992. *Structural Holes: The Social Structure of Competition*. Cambridge, MA: Harvard University Press.

Cesaroni, F., A. Di Minin, and A. Piccaluga. 2004. "New Strategic Goals and Organizational Solutions in Large R&D Labs: Lessons from Centro Ricerche Fiat and Telecom Italia Lab." *R&D Management* 34 (1): 45–56. doi:10.1111/j.1467-9310.2004.00321.x.

Charmaz, K. 2011. "Grounded Theory Methods in Social Justice Research." *The Sage Handbook of Qualitative Research* 4 (1): 359–380.

Chesbrough, H. W. 2003. *Open Innovation: The New Imperative for Creating and Profiting from Technology*. Cambridge, MA: Harvard Business Press.

Chesbrough, H. W. 2006a. *Open Business Models: How to Thrive in the New Innovation Landscape. Harvard Business Press.* 50. Harvard Business Press. http://books.google.com/books?hl=de&id=-f4XSIN37coC&pgis=1.

Chesbrough, H. W. 2006b. "Open Innovation: A New Paradigm for Understanding Industrial Innovation." In *Open Innovation: Researching a New Paradigm*, edited by H. W. Chesbrough, W. Vanhaverbeke, and J. West, 1–12. Oxford: Oxford University Press. https://doi.org/citeulike-article-id:5207447.

Chesbrough, H. W. 2015. From open science to open innovation. Institute for Innovation and Knowledge Management. ESADE. https://www.fosteropenscience.eu/content/open-science-open-innovation

Chesbrough, H. W., and A. K. Crowther. 2006. "Beyond High-Tech: Early Adopters of Open Innovation in Other Industries." *R&D Management* 36 (3): 229–236. doi:10.1111/j.1467-9310.2006.00428.x.

Chesbrough, H. W., and S. Brunswicker. 2014. "A Fad or A Phenomenon?" *Research Technology Management* 57 (2): p16–25. doi:10.5437/08956308X5702196.

Chiaroni, D., V. Chiesa, and F. Frattini. 2010. "Unravelling the Process from Closed to Open Innovation: Evidence from Mature, Asset-Intensive Industries." *R&D Management* 40 (3): 222–245. doi:10.1111/j.1467-9310.2010.00589.x.

Christensen, J. F. 2006. "Wither Core Competency for the Large Corporation in an Open Innovation World?" *Open Innovation: Researching a New Paradigm*, no. August 2005. 35–61. doi:10.1016/j.jbusvent.2009.12.002.

Cohen, W. M., and D. A. Levinthal. 1990. "Absorptive Capacity : A New Perspective on and Innovation Learning." *Administrative Science Quarterly* 35 (1): 128–152. doi:10.2307/2393553.

D'Este, P., and M. Perkmann. 2011. "Why Do Academics Engage with Industry? the Entrepreneurial University and Individual Motivations." *Journal of Technology Transfer* 36 (3): 316–339. doi:10.1007/s10961-010-9153-z.

Dahlander, L., and D. M. Gann. 2010. "How Open Is Innovation?" *Research Policy* 39 (6): 699–709. doi:10.1016/j.respol.2010.01.013.

De Marco, C. E. 2017. "The Challenges of Implementing Open Innovation. A Systematic Literature Review." PhD Dissertation, Scuola Superiore Sant'Anna, Pisa.

Dhanaraj, C., and A. Parkhe. 2006. "Innovation Networks Orchestrating." *The Academy of Management Review* 31 (3): 659–669. doi:10.1007/978-3-540-92267-4.

Di Minin, A., F. Frattini, and A. Piccaluga. 2010. "Fiat : Open Innovation in a Downtrun." *California Management Review* 52 (3): 132–160. doi:10.1525/cmr.2010.52.3.132.

Dodgson, M., D. M. Gann, and A. J. Salter. 2006. "The Role of Technology in the Shift Towards Open Innovation: The Case of Procter & Gamble." *R&D Management* 36 (3): 333–346. doi:10.1111/j.1467-9310.2006.00429.x.

Eisenhardt, K. M. 1989. "Building Theories from Case Study Research." *Academy of Management Review* 14: 532–550. doi:10.5465/amr.1989.4308385.

Eisenhardt, K. M., and M. E. Graebner. 2007. "Theory Building from Cases: Opportunities and Challenges." *Academy of Management Journal* 50 (1): 25–32. doi:10.5465/amj.2007.24160888.

Fazey, I., J. A. Fazey, J. Fischer, K. Sherren, J. Warren, R. F. Noss, and S. R. Dovers. 2007. "Adaptive Leverage Capacity for and Learning to Learn As." *Frontiers in Ecology and Environment* 5 (7): 375–380. doi:10.1890/1540-9295(2007)5[375:ACALTL]2.0.CO;2.

Gassmann, O. 2006. "Opening up the Innovation Process : Towards an Agenda." *R&D Management* 36 (3): 223–228. doi:10.1111/j.1467-9310.2006.00437.x.

Gassmann, O., and E. Enkel. 2004. "Towards a Theory of Open Innovation: Three Core Process Archetypes." *R&D Management Conference* 1–18.

Giannopoulou, E., A. Yström, and S. Ollila. 2011. "Turning Open Innovation into Practice: Open Innovation Research through the Lens of Managers." *International Journal of Innovation Management* 15 (3): 505–524. doi:10.1142/S1363919611003465.

Giddens, A. 1984. *The Construction of Society*. Cambridge, MA: Polity.

Goldkuhl, G., and S. Cronholm. 2010. "Adding Theoretical Grounding to Grounded Theory: Toward Multi-Grounded Theory." *International Journal of Qualitative Methods* 9 (2): 187–205. doi:10.1177/160940691000900205.

Hafkesbrink, J., and M. Schroll. 2010. "Organizational Competences for Open Innovation in Small and Medium Sized Enterprises of the Digital Economy." In *Competences Management for Open Innovation. Tools and IT-Support to Unlock the Innovation Potential beyond Company Boundaries*, edited by J. Hafkesbrink, U. H. Hoppe, and J. Schlichter, 21–52. Cologne, Germany: JosefEul Verlag, Lohmar Köln

Huizingh, E. K. R. E. 2011. "Open Innovation: State of the Art and Future Perspectives." *Technovation* 31 (1): 2–9. doi:10.1016/j.technovation.2010.10.002.

Huston, L., and N. Sakkab. 2006. "Connect and Develop inside Procter & Gamble's New Model for Innovation." *Harvard Business Review* 84 (3): 58–67. doi:10.1111/j.1943-278X.2010.00006.x.

Kim, B., E. Kim, and N. J. Foss. 2016. "Balancing Absorptive Capacity and Inbound Open Innovation for Sustained Innovative Performance: An Attention-Based View." *European Management Journal* 34 (1): 80–90. doi:10.1016/j.emj.2015.10.002.

Laursen, K., and A. J. Salter. 2006. "Open for Innovation: The Role of Openness in Explaining Innovation Performance among UK Manufacturing Firms." *Strategic Management Journal* 27 (2): 131–150. doi:10.1002/smj.507.

Lazzarotti, V., and R. Manzini. 2009. "Different Modes of Open Innovation: A Theoretical Framework and an Empirical Study." *International Journal of Innovation Management* 13 (4): 615–636. doi:10.1142/S1363919609002443.

Lee, S., G. Park, B. Yoon, and J. Park. 2010. "Open Innovation in SMEs—An Intermediated Network Model." *Research Policy* 39 (2): 290–300. doi:10.1016/j.respol.2009.12.009.

Lenz, S., M. Pinhanez, L. E. De Césaris, and C. Jacobs. 2016. "Open Innovation and the Challenges of Human Resource Management." *International Journal of Innovation Management* 20 (7): 1650063-01/26. doi:10.1142/S1363919616500638.

Lifshitz-Assaf, H. 2017. "Dismantling Knowledge Boundaries at NASA: The Critical Role of Professional Identity in Open Innovation." *Administrative Science Quarterly*. doi:10.1177/0001839217747876.

Lind, F., A. Styhre, and L. Aaboen. 2013. "Exploring University-Industry Collaboration in Research Centres." *European Journal of Innovation Management* 16 (1): 70–91. doi:10.1108/14601061311292869.

Maggioni, M. A., S. Breschi, and P. Panzarasa. 2013. "Multiplexity, Growth Mechanisms and Structural Variety in Scientific Collaboration Networks Multiplexity, Growth Mechanisms and Structural Variety in Scientific Collaboration Networks." *Industry and Innovation* 20 (3): 185–194. doi:10.1080/13662716.2013.791124.

Mahdad, M., A. Piccaluga, and A. Di Minin. 2015. "When Industry and University Live under the Same Roof: Telecom Italia's Joint Laboratories Initiatives". Presented in the R&D Management Conference, Pisa, Italy.

Ollila, S., and M. Elmquist. 2011. "Managing Open Innovation: Exploring Challenges at the Interfaces of an Open Innovation Arena." *Creativity & Innovation Management* 20 (4): 273–283. doi:10.1111/j.1467-8691.2011.00616.x.

Oumlil, R., and C. Juiz. 2016. "An Up-To-Date Survey in Barriers to Open Innovation." *Journal of Technology Management & Innovation* 11 (3): 137–153. doi:10.4067/S0718-27242016000300016.

Perkmann, M., and K. Walsh. 2007. "University-Industry Relationships and Open Innovation: Towards a Research Agenda." *International Journal of Management Reviews* 9 (4): 259–280. doi:10.1111/j.1468-2370.2007.00225.x.

Pichault, F. 1995. "The Management of Politics in Technically Related Organizational Change." *Organization Studies* 16 (3): 449/476. doi:10.1177/017084069501600304.

Pisano, G. P. 2015. "You Need an Innovation Strategy the Big Idea." *Harvard Business Review* 93 (June): 44–54.

Randhawa, K., R. Wilden, and J. Hohberger. 2016. "A Bibliometric Review of Open Innovation: Setting A Research Agenda." *Journal of Product Innovation Management* 33 (6): 750–772. doi:10.1111/jpim.12312.

Rindova, V. P., and S. Kotha. 2001. "Continuous 'Morphing': Competing through Dynamic Capabilities, Form, and Function." *The Academy of Management Journal* 44 (6): 1263–1280.

Roberts, J. 2000. "From Know-How to Show-How? Questioning the Role of Information and Communication Technologies in Knowledge Transfer." *Technology Analysis & Strategic Management* 12 (4): 429–443. doi:10.1080/713698499.

Rohrbeck, R., K. Hölzle, and H. G. Gemünden. 2009. "Opening up for Competitive Advantage - How Deutsche Telekom Creates an Open Innovation Ecosystem." *R&D Management* 39 (4): 420–430. doi:10.1111/j.1467-9310.2009.00568.x.

Salter, A. J., and B. R. Martin. 2001. "The Economic Benefits of Publicly Funded Basic Research: A Critical Review. R." *Research Policy* 30: 509–532. doi:10.1016/S0048-7333(00)00091-3.

Sanchez, R. 1995. "Strategic Flexibility in Product Competition." *Strategic Management Journal, Summer Special Issue* 16 (Summer Special Issue): 135–159. doi:10.1002/(ISSN)1097-0266.

Staber, U., and J. Sydow. 2002. "Organizational Adaptive Capacity: A Structuration Perspective." *Journal of Management Inquiry* 11 (4): 408–424. doi:10.1177/1056492602238848.

Teece, D. J., G. Pisano, and A. Shuen. 1997. "Dynamic Capabilities and Strategic Management." *Strategic Management Journal* 18 (7): 509–533. doi:10.1002/(SICI)1097-0266(199708)18:7<509::AID-SMJ882>3.0.CO;2-Z.

Thune, T., and M. Gulbrandsen. 2014. "Dynamics of Collaboration in University–Industry Partnerships: Do Initial Conditions Explain Development Patterns?" *Journal of Technology Transfer* 39 (6): 977–993. doi:10.1007/s10961-014-9331-5.

Traitler, H., H. J. Watzke, and I. Sam Saguy. 2011. "Reinventing R&D in an Open Innovation Ecosystem." *Journal of Food Science* 76 (2): R62–68. doi:10.1111/j.1750-3841.2010.01998.x.

van de Vrande, V., J. P. J. de Jong, W. Vanhaverbeke, and M. de Rochemont. 2009. "Open Innovation in SMEs: Trends, Motives and Management Challenges." *Technovation* 29 (6–7): 423–437. doi:10.1016/j.technovation.2008.10.001.

Vanhaverbeke, W., and M. Cloodt. 2014. "Theories of the Firm and Open Innovation." In *New Frontiers in Open Innovation*, edited by H. W. Chesbrough, W. Vanhaverbeke, and J. West, 256–278. Oxford: Oxford University Press. doi:10.1093/acprof.

Wang, C. L., and P. K. Ahmed. 2007. "Dynamic Capabilities: A Review and Research Agenda." *International Journal of Management Reviews* 9 (1): 31–51. doi:10.1111/j.1468-2370.2007.00201.x.

Wuyts, S., M. G. Colombo, S. Dutta, and B. Nooteboom. 2005. "Empirical Tests of Optimal Cognitive Distance." *Journal of Economic Behavior and Organization* 58 (2): 277–302. doi:10.1016/j.jebo.2004.03.019.

Yin, R. K. 2008. "The Case Study Crisis : Some Answers The Case Study Crisis : Some Answers *." *Administrative Science Quarterly* 26 (1): 58–65. doi:10.2307/2392599.

Zobel, A. K. 2017. "Benefiting from Open Innovation: A Multidimensional Model of Absorptive Capacity*." *Journal of Product Innovation Management* 34 (3): 269–288. doi:10.1111/jpim.12361.

# Collaborative ties and ambidextrous innovation: insights from internal and external knowledge acquisition

Xuemei Xie, Yanru Gao, Zhipeng Zang and Xiaohua Meng

**ABSTRACT**

Building collaborative ties has become an increasingly important strategy for influencing firms' ambidextrous innovation in transition economies, we examine the relationship between collaborative ties and ambidextrous innovation—with a focus on the mediating effect of knowledge acquisition using firm-level data in China. The empirical results reveal several important findings. First, collaborative ties among partners have a positive effect on firms' ambidextrous innovation. Second, collaborative ties among partners are more beneficial to the firm's external knowledge acquisition than internal knowledge acquisition. Lastly, the mediating effect of internal knowledge acquisition on the relationship between collaborative ties and ambidextrous innovation of firms is higher than that of external knowledge acquisition. These findings contribute to the literature on ambidexterity theory. Moreover, these findings also extend our understanding of the importance of the integration of internal and external knowledge acquisition in collaborative relationships, and enrich knowledge management literature within the collaborative ties framework.

## 1. Introduction

Open innovation theories discuss the fact that a single company may have difficulty achieving a competitive advantage in the current marketplace, but that individual partners could potentially reach greater innovative performance in their collaborative activities (Laursen and Salter 2006). In a fiercely competitive environment, collaboration is increasingly considered beneficial to help firms spawn innovation and competitive advantage (Dingler and Enkel 2016). Thus, establishing collaborative ties with various partners becomes an important strategy for businesses to improve their innovative activities and performance.

The concept of 'ambidexterity,' first proposed by Duncan (1976), is defined as an organization's capability to adapt to environmental changes while efficiently managing daily business. Later, this idea became much more widely accepted by scholars in the fields of management and innovation. From a technological innovation perspective, March (1991) was the first to unite the two notions of exploitation and exploration in terms of ambidexterity. Thus, ambidextrous innovation can be regarded as the ability to simultaneously pursue both exploratory and exploitative innovation strategies that require the careful allocation of a firm's resources (Agostini, Nosella, and Filippini 2016; March 1991). Here, exploratory innovation is defined as innovation activities that is related to radical change, risk taking, creativity, disruptive innovation, and entering new product market domains (He and Wong 2004; March 1991); while exploitative innovation is defined as innovation activities that is related to incremental change and improving existing product market positions (He and Wong 2004; March 1991). Thus conceptualized, exploratory innovation creates new methods or materials derived from the knowledge dimension that is novel to a given organization (Karamanos 2012; March 1991; Wang and Hsu 2014); while exploitative innovation improves existing methods or materials used by organizations to achieve their goals (Enkel and Gassmann 2010; March 1991). Overall, ambidextrous innovation has increasingly become a vital topic in the technology innovation field (Gilsing and Nooteboom 2005; Lavie, Stettner, and Tushman 2010; Wang and Hsu 2014).

Prior studies have focused on the relationships between organizations' collaboration and firms' innovative performance (e.g. Jean and Sinkovics 2010; Tomlinson 2010; Zeng, Xie, and Tam 2010), as well as ambidextrous innovation and firm performance (e.g. He and Wong 2004; Lubatkin et al. 2006). However, few studies have examined the relationship between collaborative ties and ambidextrous innovation. More specifically, little research has looked at how collaborative ties interact with other factors in the course of firms' ambidextrous innovation. In this context, knowledge acquisition is a crucial element in the link between collaborative ties and ambidextrous innovation (Lee and Yang 2014).

The concepts of external and internal knowledge are complementary types within the greater classification of 'knowledge' (Cassiman and Veugelers 2006; Cohen and Levinthal 1990). A firm's knowledge not only comes from itself but also from outside partners, both of which are necessary for the company's development. However, the excessive dominance of one of them will generate a negative effect (Raisch et al. 2009). Further, because of the small amount of transference of internal knowledge (Frenz and Ietto-Gillies 2009), firms could supplement external knowledge with internal capabilities, transfer knowledge internally, and promote internal knowledge renewal (Liao and Marsillac 2015). In this paper, we discuss the classification of internal and external knowledge as they pertain to business success.

Accordingly, knowledge acquisition is divided into external knowledge acquisition and internal knowledge acquisition (Frenz and Ietto-Gillies 2009). Firms can make full use of both to drive their respective innovation processes, as well as to gain potential opportunities and advantages by leveraging the relationship between knowledge and innovation (Martinez-Torres and Olmedilla 2016). Moreover, establishing collaborative ties between firms and their partners may be a critical way for companies to move forward with innovative ideas using the enrichment of their knowledge base (Lee and Yang 2014). Prior researchers have investigated the impacts of knowledge acquisition on firms' performances (e.g. Hung and Chou 2013; Lin and Wu 2010), innovative performances (e.g. Isaksson, Simeth, and Seifert 2016), new product development (e.g. Frankort 2016; Yli-Renko, Autio, and Sapizenza 2001), and especially external knowledge acquisition (e.g. Liao et al. 2009; Liao and Marsillac 2015). However, until recently, few studies have examined the impacts of knowledge acquisition on exploratory or exploitative innovation (e.g. Bierly, Damanpour, and Santoro 2009).

Based on the research gaps identified in the existing literature, this paper is designed to examine the relationship between collaborative ties and ambidextrous innovation using a sample of 323 manufacturing firms in China, which further enriches the notion of network theory from the perspective of ambidexterity. Second, this paper examines the mediating effect of knowledge acquisition on the relationship between collaborative ties and ambidextrous innovation, which further reveals the internal mechanism between collaboration and ambidextrous innovation. Therefore, this work extends the existing literature on ambidextrous innovation from the perspectives of collaborative ties and knowledge acquisition.

## 2. Theories and hypotheses

Collaboration is a complex and multidimensional process characterized by many constructs, including coordination, communication, relationships, and trust (Kotlarsky and Oshri 2005). From a business perspective, collaborative ties refer to the contact that firms have with their partners such as customers and suppliers, which can reduce transaction costs by (a) building trust and enhancing communications (Li et al. 2013), (b) contributing to the cross-fertilization of ideas, and (c) enabling the combination of different pieces of knowledge to create something new and useful (Wang 2016). Collaborative ties are usually built among firms when they do not have all the necessary resources at their disposal (including knowledge), and when they wish to share the costs and risks in the process of innovation (Tether 2002). Moreover, collaborative ties may provide firms sufficient market information from partners (e.g. customers, suppliers, agents, etc.), which makes it easier for them to transform resources from an environment into one that has knowledge learning and relevant innovation (Li et al. 2013).

From a resource-based view (RBV), the key idea behind collaborative ties is that firms can benefit from collaboration in terms of production, organization, and the transfer of crucial knowledge through the exchange and coordination of resources and information, thus leading to greater levels of both products and process innovations (Tomlinson 2010). In so doing, they have a greater ability to achieve further, sustained competitive advantages in the marketplace (Jean and Sinkovics 2010). As mentioned, according to ambidexterity theory, exploratory innovation is a revolutionary change while exploitative innovation improves existing methods or materials (March 1991). Whichever type of innovation mode or modes that are adopted, necessary resources and proper information acquisition is essential to firms. As an important channel for companies to acquire resources (Lenz-Cesar and Heshmati 2012; Sharif, Baark, and Lau 2012), building collaborative ties with partners has positive impacts on the implementation of both exploratory and exploitative innovation activities (Guan and Liu 2016; Hernández-Espallardo, Sánchez-Pérez, and Segovia-López 2011).

In addition, knowledge, as the fundamental driver of value creation for a firm (Scott-Kennel and Giroud 2015), and its acquisition is also critical for a company's long-term development (Moorthy and Polley 2010; Zack 1999). At first, innovation is embedded in knowledge networks (Purchase, Olaru, and Denize 2014; Wang et al. 2014), and the flow of knowledge can help firms integrate and coordinate partners' technological knowledge and information, thereby promoting innovative performance (Zhao, Xi, and Yi 2015). In this case, knowledge acquisition in innovation relies on interactions with various knowledge sources (Parker 2012; Yli-Renko, Autio, and Sapizenza 2001). Each individual can gain some knowledge in his or her own way through their interactions, and then incorporate that knowledge into their own perspectives, which enriches the diversity of the firm's existing knowledge base (López-Sáez et al. 2010). Accordingly, building collaborative ties with partners can help firms expand the sources of knowledge acquisition, obtain complementary resources, reduce innovation costs, and improve the successful rate of innovation (Karamanos 2012). Therefore, knowledge acquisition is a mediating factor for the relationship between collaborative ties and ambidextrous innovation (Bierly, Damanpour, and Santoro 2009).

Based on this view, and according to both RBV and network theory, businesses can obtain the knowledge they need by building collaborative ties with different partners and further promoting their ambidextrous innovation activities. A conceptual model of this idea is provided in Figure 1, which shows the close relationships among collaborative ties, knowledge acquisition, and ambidextrous innovation. It is assumed that there are positive relationships between the collaborative ties and the ambidextrous innovation of firms. Moreover, it is presumed that knowledge acquisition mediate the relationship between the collaborative ties and the ambidextrous innovation of firms. We next propose our hypotheses concerning the relationships that exist among the variables.

### *2.1. Collaborative ties and ambidextrous innovation*

Since March (1991) first embedded ambidexterity theory into the technological innovation field, the concept of ambidextrous innovation, which has been emphasized to a firm's capacity to simultaneously leverage exploratory innovation and exploitative innovation (Agostini, Nosella, and Filippini 2016; Cao, Gedajlovic, and Zhang 2009; Zang and Li 2017), has received greater attention by scholars. However, in practice, there is a tension or 'trade-offs' between exploration and exploitation, because they are fundamentally different logics that compete for scarce resources, require very different

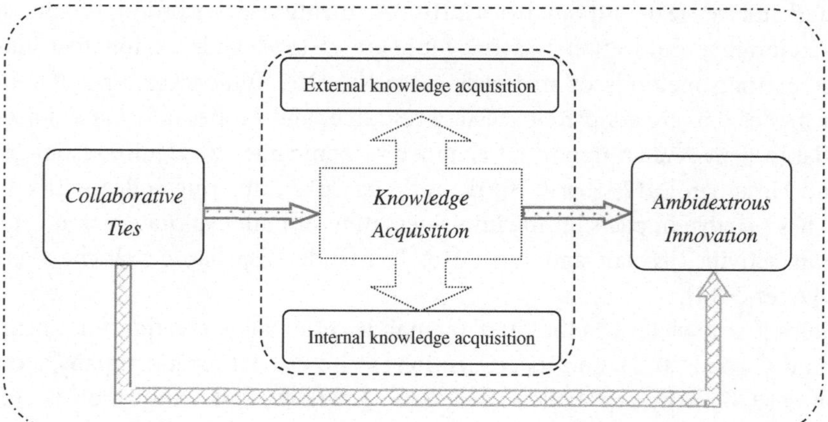


**Figure 1.** Conceptual model.

strategies and structures, and orient the organization in the pursuit of different goals (He and Wong 2004; March 1991; Tushman and O'Reilly 1996). According to the RBV, the nature of the ambidexterity is contingent on the firm's available resources – the amount of resources that the firm possesses or can readily access from outside the firm (Cao, Gedajlovic, and Zhang 2009). When firms have access to sufficient resources, trade-offs between exploratory innovation and exploitative innovation may not be binding constraints.

Thus, overcoming the challenges associated with compensating for an inability to exploit or explore may require the use of external mechanisms (Dunlap et al. 2016). Considering the important role of interacting with a broader set of collaborators play in innovation (Rossi, Caloffi, and Russo 2016), building collaborative ties represent the external mechanisms that have the potential to overcome these challenges.

First, according to the dynamic capabilities (DC) theory, exploratory innovation is the process of developing new capabilities to seek more opportunities (Lavie, Stettner, and Tushman 2010), including pursuing new knowledge, discovering breakthrough ideas, and developing new products or services (Zang and Li 2017). Close collaborative ties which refer to firms' high levels of interactions with their partners, can benefit explorative innovation through helping firms acquire new knowledge and information, and further contributing to the generation of new ideas through their interactions (Dingler and Enkel 2016; Tomlinson 2010). Furthermore, close collaborative ties with partners can help firms engage in new, exploratory types of product innovations (Dunlap et al. 2016), address new problems through exploratory innovation (Im and Rai 2008), and reduce costs and potential risks in innovation process (Demirkan and Demirkan 2012; Karamanos 2012).

Second, in line with the RBV, exploitation is the process of utilizing the firm's internal resources and allocating the resources to improve the existing products and processes (March 1991). Due to the characteristics of exploitation, building collaborative ties between firms and their partners offers firms the opportunity to gain access to a wider range of knowledge resources that is complementary to the firms' extant knowledge base, hence enlarging and diversifying their pool of resources (Rosenkopf and Almeida 2003), which will facilitate exploitative innovation.

In sum, we reason that the tension between exploratory innovation and exploitative innovation may be relatively less for firms with close collaborative ties, because a wider range of resource bases provide firms a better buffer to mitigate the risks associated with an unbalanced pursuit of exploration and exploitation. Thus, close collaborative ties can help firms to develop both exploratory and exploitative innovations so that improve firms' ambidextrous innovation. Therefore, we hypothesize that:

Hypothesis 1: Close collaborative ties between firms and their partners are more likely to help firms to carry out ambidextrous innovation activities.

### *2.2. Collaborative ties and knowledge acquisition*

The knowledge-based view (KBV) highlights the facts that knowledge is the most strategically significant resource of a firm and that the ability to generate, absorb and exploit knowledge is essential to a firm's ability to innovate (Grant 1996). However, firms usually do not have all the knowledge they require, and they need to acquire knowledge by having ties outside the firms (Parra-Requena et al. 2015). Given that knowledge acquisition relies on interactions with knowledge sources (Liao and Marsillac 2015), establishing collaborative ties with partners is regarded as an effective approach for the creation, transfer, and sharing of knowledge (Sun 2016). In this regards, collaborative ties can serve as a major external source for knowledge acquisition (Ahuja 2000; Karamanos 2012). Therefore, we posit that the extent of a firm's collaboration with its partners will be related to its level of external and internal knowledge acquisition.

First, firms having collaboration with a variety of external partners can be seen as a major mechanism through which firms acquire external knowledge (Chen and Tan 2016; Laursen and Salter 2006). On the one hand, close collaboration relationships enable the firm to gain multi-channel access to a larger variety of new knowledge resources from external partners (Chang, Bai, and Li 2015; Grimpe and Kaiser 2010). On the other hand, given that external knowledge acquisition generally requires longer and extensive interpersonal relationship and trust (Kong 2015), and a high level of trust can facilitate the exchange of confidential information and the share of valuable knowledge (Parra-Requena et al. 2015), close collaborative ties allows firms to better identify, acquire, and utilize external knowledge appropriately by building trust among partners.

Second, collaboration is essentially an exchange or sharing of knowledge and resources between collaborating partners (Chen and Tan 2016). The key to an effective internal knowledge acquisition is, first, to acquire knowledge effectively. For one thing, internal knowledge acquisition usually depends on a firm's knowledge base. In this respect, close collaboration can help firms access a larger variety of knowledge resources from external partners (Grimpe and Kaiser 2010), hence facilitating a constant flow of external knowledge into internal organizational learning processes. For another, as a collaborative process is composed of extensive knowledge flow among employees of different partners (Ma and Huang 2016), the knowledge acquired from outside partners enables employees within a firm to deepen their thinking and to advance their innovative ideas (Chang, Bai, and Li 2015). Therefore, firms can complement their own resources and knowledge base in the process of collaborative value creation with resources and knowledge acquired from the outside (Grant and Baden-Fuller 2004). Overall, a firm can create knowledge internally from external ideas or information (Forés and Camisón 2016).

Moreover, building collaborative ties can promote the exchange and sharing of a company's private knowledge, as each firm can potentially receive a greater amount of knowledge via collaborations, thus facilitating the integration of complementary knowledge (Ahuja 2000; He, Ghobadian, and Gallear 2013). Further, collaborative ties as the contact that firms have with their partners can help firms to combine different external knowledge to create something new and useful (Li et al. 2013; Wang 2016). Thus, close collaborative ties with partners may be more beneficial to external knowledge acquisition than internal knowledge acquisition. Therefore, we propose that:

Hypothesis 2: Close collaborative ties between a firm and their partners are more beneficial to the firm's external knowledge acquisition than internal knowledge acquisition.

### 2.3. The mediating effect of knowledge acquisition

In the existing literature, some studies have realized the impact of collaborative ties on ambidextrous innovation (e.g. Hernández-Espallardo, Sánchez-Pérez, and Segovia-López 2011); whether some mediating factors have additional effects on collaborative relationships remains absent from the research. Some previous work has revealed that there are close links between collaborative ties and knowledge acquisition (Chen and Tan 2016; Raisch et al. 2009) while other studies have suggested that knowledge acquisition influences firms' exploratory and exploitative innovation activities (Wang and Hsu 2014). From this, we can see that knowledge acquisition is a vital factor for the implementation of the ambidextrous innovation activities of firms (Guan and Liu 2016). Following this line of argument, we regard knowledge acquisition as a key explanatory mechanism mediating between collaborative ties and ambidextrous innovation.

For one thing, external knowledge, which is closely associated with the richness of a firm's existing knowledge base (Gupta and Govindarajan 2000), can help companies increase their innovation productivity (Laursen and Salter 2006). Close collaborative ties which are a benefit for a firm's external knowledge acquisition, can provide the firm with novel knowledge resources (Ahuja 2000; Grimpe and Kaiser 2010), hence benefiting explorative innovation through enabling firms to possess an irreplaceable advantage in introducing novel products and entering new markets. Therefore, firms can strengthen their ability to conduct exploratory innovation through external knowledge gained from collaboration to generate novel ideas (Katila and Ahuja 2002; March 1991).

For another, according to the RBV, the antecedents of exploitative innovation are resources and capabilities which favor firms' internal improvement (He and Wong 2004; Marín-Idárraga, Hurtado González, and Cabello Medina 2016). The repeated use of existing knowledge is regarded as a critical aspect of exploitative innovation (Wang and Hsu 2014). In this respect, collaborative ties could enlarge and diversify firms' pool of resources by effective external knowledge acquisition (Rosenkopf and Almeida 2003), which will facilitate firms' engagement in exploitative innovation. Moreover, internal knowledge acquisition renews a firm's knowledge stock and promotes the firm's internal knowledge creation through the combination of external knowledge and the exchange of employees' private professional knowledge (Forés and Camisón 2016). Overall, combining the knowledge acquired from the outside with an existing knowledge base is useful for exploitative innovation (Guan and Liu 2016).

Moreover, we posit that internal knowledge acquisition may have greater mediating effect on the relationship between collaborative ties and ambidextrous innovation than that of external knowledge acquisition. First, compared to external knowledge acquisition, internal knowledge acquisition can create more knowledge through the absorption, assimilation, and utilization of external knowledge (Cohen and Levinthal 1990). Second, internal knowledge acquisition can strengthen a company's abilities to utilize knowledge, and foster a company's ability for continuous innovation (Estrada, Faems, and Faria 2016). Third, internal knowledge acquisition can be more beneficial for facilitating knowledge mobility and the sharing of information among departments and individuals within a firm than external knowledge acquisition, so that can help firms to better incorporate external knowledge from collaborative ties into firms' ambidextrous innovation. Hence, we hypothesize that:

Hypothesis 3: The mediating effect of internal knowledge acquisition on the relationship between collaborative ties and ambidextrous innovation of firms is greater than that of external knowledge acquisition.

## 3. Methods

### 3.1. Data source

The data was collected using a survey method. The topics include firms' collaborative ties, knowledge acquisition, and ambidextrous innovation. In the survey, we chose the manufacturing companies of 27 industrial sectors located in sixteen cities around the Yangtze Delta Region of China, including Shanghai, Jiangsu Province, and Zhejiang Province, where the most developed Chinese manufacturing industries are located as the survey population. First, we conducted a pilot by sending semi-opened questionnaires to 30 companies and modified according to the feedback of the respondents at these companies. We then conducted the full survey by using closed-end questionnaire. Thus, questionnaires were sent to 650 manufacturing companies that were randomly selected from a stratified sample based on the size (4 types) and industries of firms (27 sectors). The questionnaires were mainly sent to those senior managers, department managers, and R&D personnel in companies who had a rich experience in knowledge management and innovation processes. Finally, of the 650 questionnaires that were sent out, we received 323 valid responses, providing a response rate of 49.69%.

To test for non-response bias, we compared the first and fourth quartiles of responses for differences on the dependent and independent variables (Armstrong and Overton 1977). Results shown in Table A1 suggest that the calculated t-statistics for the collaborative ties ($t = -0.816$, $p = 0.416$), external knowledge acquisition ($t = -0.867$, $p = 0.387$), internal knowledge acquisition ($t = -0.595$, $p = 0.553$), exploratory innovation ($t = -0.643$, $p = 0.521$), and exploitative innovation ($t = -0.557$, $p = 0.579$) were all statistically insignificant ($p > 0.05$). Moreover, we conducted $F$ tests to make the comparison between responded and non-responded firms using industry and firm size. The results in Table A2 did not show significant differences ($p > 0.05$). Thus, the non-response bias was not a concern in this study.

In addition, some methods were used to reduce common method bias (CMB) in this research (Podsakoff et al. 2003). First, during the survey process, we told the respondents that the questionnaire was anonymous. Second, we made the questionnaire statements simple, clear, and easy to understand. Third, the Harman's single-factor test showed that the first factor explaining was 21.37%, revealing that CMB was not a concern in this study.

As for the sample characteristics, there are 38.70% private enterprises (PEs); 28.17% state-owned enterprises (SOEs); 25.39% foreign-invested enterprises (FIEs); and 7.74% collectively-run enterprises (CREs). 40.25% of the firms had between 20 and 300 employees. Approximately 87% of the firms have had an annual turnover of over 3 million *yuan* in the past three years. About 35% of the firms have been in operation for more than 15 years. The two largest industrial sectors selected in our study were 'computers, communications and electronic equipment' (13.62%) and 'textiles and garments' (12.07%) (Figure A1).

### 3.2. Measures

#### 3.2.1. Collaborative ties

Following prior studies (Inemek and Matthyssens 2013; Yang et al. 2008), collaborative ties, which reflect the close collaborative relationships among firms and their partners (including customers, suppliers, agents, and so forth), were measured using four items in the present study (see Table 1). In the survey, the respondents were asked to indicate the extent of their approval regarding the collaborative ties of their firms, and the items for the construct were assessed using a 7-point Likert scale (ranging from 1 = '*strongly disagree*' to 7 = '*strongly agree*').

#### 3.2.2. Knowledge acquisition

According to Chen and Huang (2009), knowledge acquisition is essential to promote a firm's knowledge management capability. In this study, knowledge acquisition was measured using the two constructs of external knowledge acquisition and internal

**Table 1.** Variables and measurements.

| Variables | Items | Sources |
|---|---|---|
| Collaborative ties (CT) | CT1. Close coordination and cooperation with partners.<br>CT2. Spend a higher amount of time and effort with partners.<br>CT3. Willing to continue relationships with partners.<br>CT4. Have trust-based relationships with partners. | Inemek and Matthyssens (2013);<br>Yang et al. (2008) |
| External knowledge acquisition (EA) | EA1. Knowledge is obtained from suppliers.<br>EA2. Knowledge is obtained from customers.<br>EA3. Knowledge is obtained from other agents. | Chen and Huang (2009) |
| Internal knowledge acquisition (IA) | IA1. Knowledge is obtained from the communication between supervisors and subordinates.<br>IA2. Knowledge is obtained from the communication among colleagues.<br>IA3. Knowledge is obtained from other departments within the firm. | Chen and Huang (2009) |
| Exploratory innovation (ER) | ER1. Acquire manufacturing technologies and skills entirely new to the firm.<br>ER2. Open up new markets.<br>ER3. Acquire entirely new managerial and organizational skills that are important for innovation.<br>ER4. Enter new technology fields and introduce new generations of products. | Atuahene-Gima (2005); He and Wong (2004) |
| Exploitative innovation (EI) | EI1. Invest mainly in enhancing skills and mature technologies.<br>EI2. Target efforts on improving the efficiency of innovation processes rather than on initiating new ventures radically different from what the firms are familiar with.<br>EI3. Reduce production costs and the consumption of materials.<br>EI4. Base strategies on the knowledge and abilities the firm is already familiar with, and then search for solutions to customer problems that are near to existing solutions, rather than searching for completely new solutions. | Atuahene-Gima (2005); He and Wong (2004) |
| Control variables | CO1. Firm size is measured in terms of the number of employees, using four dummy variables.<br>CO2. Firm age is measured by the number of years that the company had been listed by the local Industrial and Commercial Bureau at the end of the survey year, using five dummy variables.<br>CO3. Ownership includes four types: SOEs, CREs, PEs, and FIEs, which is measured using four dummy variables.<br>CO4. Industries belong to 27 subsectors, which are measured using 27 dummy variables.<br>CO5. R&D capabilities were measured by the ability to develop new products by exploiting R&D investment (1 = 'much worse than competitors' to 5 = 'much better than competitors'). | He and Wong 2004; Lin et al. 2016; Rubera, Chandrasekaran, and Ordanini 2016; Tomlinson and Fai 2016 |

knowledge acquisition, and each type of knowledge acquisition included three items (see Table 1). Similarly, the respondents were asked to indicate the amount of knowledge their firms had obtained either from within the company or from outside the company. The items for the constructs were assessed using a 7-point Likert scale (ranging from 1 = '*very little*' to 7 = '*very much*').

### 3.2.3. Ambidextrous innovation

In this study, ambidextrous innovation was an integrative construct of exploratory innovation and exploitative innovation. Following previous studies (Atuahene-Gima 2005; He and Wong 2004), both exploratory innovation and exploitative innovation were measured using a four-item scale. Here, the respondents were asked to indicate the degree to which they agreed with specific items (see Table 1) regarding the ambidextrous innovation activities of their respective companies over the past three years. The items for the constructs were assessed with a 7-point Likert scale (ranging from 1 = '*strongly disagree*' to 7 = '*strongly agree*').

Previous studies have used the combined dimension (i.e. CD) and the balance dimension (i.e. BD) to measure ambidexterity (Cao, Gedajlovic, and Zhang 2009; He and Wong 2004). The former is measured by the product of exploratory innovation and exploitative innovation, while the later dimension is measured by the absolute difference between the scores of exploratory innovation and exploitative innovation (Cao, Gedajlovic, and Zhang 2009; He and Wong 2004). However, neither CD nor BD can explain the ambidextrous innovation completely. Thus, following Zang and Li (2017), we used the following formula to measure the ambidextrous innovation (i.e. Equation (1)). Where $x_{explor}$ and $x_{exploi}$denote exploratory innovation and exploitative innovation, respectively. $|x_{explor} - x_{exploi}|$ and $x_{explor} \times x_{exploi}$represent the BD and CD, respectively. The higher the score is, the higher the level of ambidextrous innovation is.

$$Ambidextrousinnovation = f(x_{explor}, x_{exploi}) = \frac{(7 - |x_{explor} - x_{exploi}|) \times \sqrt{x_{explor} \times x_{exploi}}}{7} \quad (1)$$

### 3.2.4. Control variables

To exclude possible confounding effects, we introduced firm size and firm age into our study as control variables using a set of dummies, which were widely used in prior researches on innovation (e.g. He and Wong 2004; Lin et al. 2016; Tomlinson and Fai 2016). To control for the ownership and industry, 4 dummy variables for ownership and 27 dummy variables for industrial sectors were also created (e.g. Tomlinson and Fai 2016). Besides, given that collaborative ties and ambidextrous innovation may be determined by a firm's R&D capabilities or R&D investment (Rothaermel and Alexandre 2009; Rubera, Chandrasekaran, and Ordanini 2016), to avoid the endogeneity concern, we controlled for the effect of a firm's R&D capabilities on collaborative ties and ambidextrous innovation practices. Adapted from Rubera, Chandrasekaran, and Ordanini (2016), R&D capabilities were measured by 'the ability to develop new products by exploiting R&D investment'. In the survey, the respondents were asked to indicate their firms' R&D capabilities relative to their major competitors, and the item was assessed using a 5-point Likert scale (ranging from 1 = '*much worse than competitors*' to 5 = '*much better than competitors*').

## 4. Results

Table 2 provides the descriptive statistics, including the means (Mean), standard deviations (SD), and correlations for all the variables. It demonstrates that collaborative ties and knowledge acquisition are significantly correlated with ambidextrous innovation.

In addition, we conducted several tests to gauge each construct's reliability and validity. Table 3 illustrates the results of the reliability of the scales, including the internal consistencies (Cronbach's alpha), corrected item-total correlation (CITC), and composite reliability (CR). These results show that the values of Cronbach's alpha, CITC, and CR for each construct are all greater than 0.70, indicating an acceptable level of reliability (Fornell and Larcker 1981). In addition, the results in Table 3 illustrate the validity of the scales, including factor loadings, cumulative variance, Kaiser-Meyer-Olkin (KMO), and average variance extracted (AVE). This table shows that the values of KMO and factor loadings for the constructs are all greater than 0.70, demonstrating that the scales have high construct validity (Tabachnick and Fidell 2007). Furthermore, the AVE values are all greater than 0.5, revealing acceptable convergent validity of each construct (Fornell and Larcker 1981).

To test our hypotheses, we employed a weighted least squares analysis (WLS) to examine the explanatory power of each set of variables (Cohen et al. 2003). Compared with the general multiple regression analysis, WLS takes the sampling structure and weights into account in the process of regression (Rabe-Hesketh and Skrondal 2006). Table 4 reveals the results of the regression analyses, with ambidextrous innovation and knowledge acquisition acting as dependent variables respectively from Model 1 to Model 8. Models 1, 5, and 7, as the baseline models, included only the control variables of ownership, firm size, firm age, industry, and R&D capabilities. Next, collaborative ties and knowledge acquisition were added to the model to test their effects on the ambidextrous innovation, and to further explore the mediating effect of knowledge acquisition on the relationship between collaborative ties and ambidextrous innovation.

In Table 4, Model 2 presents the significant impact of collaborative ties on ambidextrous innovation. Thus, Hypothesis 1 is supported. The result reveals that close collaborative ties contributes to helping firms carry out ambidextrous innovation activities (Hernández-Espallardo, Sánchez-Pérez, and Segovia-López 2011). The results of Models 6 and 8 reveal that collaborative ties have positive and significant impacts on the two types of knowledge acquisition (i.e. external knowledge and internal knowledge). Thus, companies building close collaborative ties with their partners is seen as an effective strategy to promote both their internal and external knowledge acquisition (Park 2010). Furthermore, we find that the impact of collaborative ties on internal knowledge acquisition is somewhat smaller than that of external knowledge acquisition. Thus, Hypothesis 2 is supported.

Moreover, we tested the mediating effect using the three-step test proposed by Baron and Kenny (1986). The results in Table 4 show that the regression coefficients of collaborative ties in Models 3 and 4 are all significant but lower than that of Model 2.

**Table 2.** Results of correlation analyses.

| Variables | 1 | 2 | 3 | 4 | 5 | 6 | 7 | 8 | 9 | 10 | 11 | 12 | 13 | 14 | 15 | 16 | 17 | 18 |
|---|---|---|---|---|---|---|---|---|---|---|---|---|---|---|---|---|---|---|
| 1. Ownership 1 | 1.000 | | | | | | | | | | | | | | | | | |
| 2. Ownership 2 | −0.181** | 1.000 | | | | | | | | | | | | | | | | |
| 3. Ownership 3 | −0.498** | −0.230** | 1.000 | | | | | | | | | | | | | | | |
| 4. Ownership 4 | −0.365** | −0.169** | −0.463** | 1.000 | | | | | | | | | | | | | | |
| 5. Size 1 | −0.072 | 0.082 | 0.115* | −0.104 | 1.000 | | | | | | | | | | | | | |
| 6. Size 2 | −0.219** | −0.167** | 0.489** | −0.218** | −0.147** | 1.000 | | | | | | | | | | | | |
| 7. Size 3 | −0.085 | 0.216** | −0.308** | 0.300** | −0.135* | −0.619** | 1.000 | | | | | | | | | | | |
| 8. Size 4 | 0.400** | −0.089 | −0.277** | −0.049 | −0.091 | −0.416** | −0.382** | 1.000 | | | | | | | | | | |
| 9. Age 1 | 0.044 | −0.010 | 0.062 | −0.109 | 0.256** | 0.118* | −0.101 | −0.132* | 1.000 | | | | | | | | | |
| 10. Age 2 | −0.063 | 0.057 | 0.231** | −0.229** | 0.035 | 0.143** | −0.030 | −0.153** | −0.123* | 1.000 | | | | | | | | |
| 11. Age 3 | −0.172** | 0.100 | 0.156** | −0.058 | −0.062 | 0.224** | −0.020 | −0.222** | −0.182** | −0.227** | 1.000 | | | | | | | |
| 12. Age 4 | −0.055 | −0.043 | −0.034 | 0.122* | −0.083 | −0.165** | 0.107 | 0.108 | −0.145** | −0.181** | −0.268** | 1.000 | | | | | | |
| 13. Age 5 | 0.219** | −0.091 | −0.316** | 0.184** | −0.056 | −0.245** | 0.014 | 0.304** | −0.230** | −0.287** | −0.424** | −0.340** | 1.000 | | | | | |
| 14. R&D Cap. | 0.111* | 0.262** | −0.286** | 0.045 | 0.024 | −0.226** | 0.131* | 0.108 | −0.061 | 0.064 | −0.228** | 0.079 | 0.135* | 1.000 | | | | |
| 15. CT | 0.041 | 0.066 | −0.161** | 0.098 | −0.052 | −0.001 | 0.064 | −0.053 | −0.173** | −0.061 | −0.196** | 0.108 | 0.238** | 0.321** | 1.000 | | | |
| 16. EA | 0.070 | 0.059 | −0.304** | 0.231** | 0.036 | −0.094 | 0.081 | 0.003 | −0.106 | −0.137* | −0.262** | 0.138* | 0.289** | 0.332** | 0.788** | 1.000 | | |
| 17. IA | −0.007 | 0.202** | −0.280** | 0.197** | −0.021 | −0.058 | 0.115* | −0.057 | −0.177** | −0.121* | −0.106 | 0.103 | 0.207** | 0.262** | 0.749** | 0.732** | 1.000 | |
| 18. AI | 0.101 | 0.154** | −0.289** | 0.125* | −0.054 | −0.049 | 0.027 | 0.050 | −0.111* | −0.091 | −0.284** | 0.087 | 0.320** | 0.349** | 0.721** | 0.676** | 0.709** | 1.000 |
| Mean | 0.280 | 0.080 | 0.390 | 0.250 | 0.030 | 0.400 | 0.360 | 0.200 | 0.090 | 0.130 | 0.250 | 0.180 | 0.350 | 2.350 | 4.910 | 4.800 | 4.920 | 4.332 |
| S.D. | 0.451 | 0.268 | 0.488 | 0.436 | 0.173 | 0.491 | 0.481 | 0.404 | 0.286 | 0.340 | 0.434 | 0.382 | 0.478 | 1.114 | 0.987 | 0.997 | 0.998 | 1.123 |
| Min | 0 | 0 | 0 | 0 | 0 | 0 | 0 | 0 | 0 | 0 | 0 | 0 | 0 | 1.000 | 2.750 | 2.333 | 2.333 | 2.159 |
| Max | 1.000 | 1.000 | 1.000 | 1.000 | 1.000 | 1.000 | 1.000 | 1.000 | 1.000 | 1.000 | 1.000 | 1.000 | 1.000 | 7.000 | 7.000 | 7.000 | 7.000 | 7.000 |

The dummies for the 27 industrial sectors of the sample are not reported in this table. * $p < 0.1$; ** $p < 0.05$; *** $p < 0.01$. N = 323, two-tailed.

**Table 3.** Reliability and validity of scale constructs.

| Latent variables | Observed variables | KMO | Bartlett's test Approx. $\chi^2$ | df | Sig. | Cronbach's α | CITC | AVE | CR | Cumulative variance |
|---|---|---|---|---|---|---|---|---|---|---|
| Collaborative ties (CT) | CT1 | 0.829 | 624.957 | 6 | 0.000 | 0.872 | 0.849 | 0.613 | 0.825 | 72.407% |
| | CT2 | | | | | | | | | |
| | CT3 | | | | | | | | | |
| | CT4 | | | | | | | | | |
| External knowledge acquisition (EA) | EA1 | 0.726 | 374.860 | 3 | 0.000 | 0.835 | 0.814 | 0.624 | 0.791 | 75.276% |
| | EA2 | | | | | | | | | |
| | EA3 | | | | | | | | | |
| Internal knowledge acquisition (IA) | IA1 | 0.717 | 341.913 | 3 | 0.000 | 0.818 | 0.825 | 0.601 | 0.771 | 73.604% |
| | IA2 | | | | | | | | | |
| | IA3 | | | | | | | | | |
| Exploratory innovation (ER) | ER1 | 0.822 | 660.417 | 6 | 0.000 | 0.876 | 0.798 | 0.640 | 0.782 | 73.139% |
| | ER2 | | | | | | | | | |
| | ER3 | | | | | | | | | |
| | ER4 | | | | | | | | | |
| Exploitative innovation (EI) | EI1 | 0.805 | 536.600 | 6 | 0.000 | 0.847 | 0.850 | 0.587 | 0.827 | 68.695% |
| | EI2 | | | | | | | | | |
| | EI3 | | | | | | | | | |
| | EI4 | | | | | | | | | |

Thus, these results reveal that both external knowledge acquisition and internal knowledge acquisition partially mediate the relationship between collaborative ties and ambidextrous innovation. A possible reason is that the relationship between collaborative ties and ambidextrous innovation may be also affected by some other mediating mechanisms, such as firms' absorptive capacity. Further, our findings show that the mediating effect of internal knowledge acquisition on the relationship between collaborative ties and ambidextrous innovation of firms is greater than that of external knowledge acquisition. Thus, Hypothesis 3 is supported.

Moreover, we plotted the results of the mediating effects of external and internal knowledge acquisition on the relationship between collaborative ties and ambidextrous innovation using a 3-D graph. From Figure 2, we can see that when the internal knowledge acquisition is added in the linear relationship of collaborative ties and ambidextrous innovation, the slope of collaborative ties on ambidextrous innovation is flatter than that of external knowledge acquisition, which indicates that the mediating effect of internal knowledge acquisition on the relationship between collaborative ties and ambidextrous innovation of firms is greater than that of external knowledge acquisition. Overall, the result further verifies Hypothesis 3.

Given that the three-step test has low test effectiveness, we used the bootstrapping method, a nonparametric resampling procedure that does not impose the assumption of normality of the sampling distribution, to test mediation further (Preacher and Hayes 2008). According to Edwards and Lambert (2007), we bootstrapped 5,000 samples and adopted the bootstrap estimates to construct bias-corrected confidence intervals (CIs) for mediation tests in this study. The results in Table 5 show that collaborative ties have indirect effects on ambidextrous innovation via external knowledge acquisition ($b$ = 0.097; 95% bias-corrected CI: [0.007, 0.205]). Similarly, the results in Table 5 show that collaborative ties have indirect effects on ambidextrous innovation via

**Table 4.** Results of weighted least squares (WLS) regression.

| | Ambidextrous innovation | | | | External knowledge acquisition | | Internal knowledge acquisition | |
|---|---|---|---|---|---|---|---|---|
| Variables | Model 1 | Model 2 | Model 3 | Model 4 | Model 5 | Model 6 | Model 7 | Model 8 |
| *Controls* | | | | | | | | |
| Ownership 1 | 0.482***(0.162) | 0.199(0.131) | 0.233*(0.127) | 0.181(0.119) | 0.230(0.141) | 0.027(0.095) | 0.501***(0.156) | – |
| Ownership 2 | 0.909***(0.218) | 0.762***(0.174) | 0.717***(0.181) | 0.406**(0.177) | 0.276(0.202) | 0.168(0.136) | 0.966***(0.211) | 0.544***(0.155) |
| Ownership 3 | – | – | – | – | – | – | – | −0.236**(0.113) |
| Ownership 4 | 0.663***(0.165) | 0.408***(0.133) | 0.386***(0.132) | 0.235*(0.124) | 0.547***(0.143) | 0.374***(0.097) | 0.803***(0.160) | 0.315***(0.104) |
| Firm size 1 | −0.396*(0.221) | −0.362**(0.176) | −0.265(0.245) | −0.294(0.228) | 0.214(0.272) | 0.523***(0.187) | 0.210(0.213) | 0.282**(0.124) |
| Firm size 2 | – | – | – | – | – | 0.137(0.087) | – | – |
| Firm size 3 | −0.657***(0.148) | −0.433***(0.119) | −0.412***(0.116) | −0.340***(0.109) | −0.372***(0.128) | – | −0.417***(0.143) | −0.126(0.104) |
| Firm size 4 | −0.581***(0.184) | −0.253*(0.148) | −0.084(0.152) | −0.038(0.143) | −0.590***(0.166) | 0.017(0.105) | −0.388**(0.177) | 0.074(0.123) |
| 5 dummies for firm age | added | added | added | added | added | added | added | added |
| 27 dummies for industries | added | added | added | added | added | added | added | added |
| R&D capabilities | 0.205***(0.054) | 0.041(0.045) | 0.006(0.046) | 0.042(0.043) | 0.255***(0.049) | 0.078**(0.034) | 0.107**(0.052) | −0.084**(0.036) |
| *Predictors* | | | | | | | | |
| CT | | 0.640***(0.050) | 0.576***(0.074) | 0.391***(0.063) | | 0.693***(0.037) | | 0.690***(0.042) |
| EA | | | 0.140*(0.079) | | | | | |
| IA | | | | 0.399***(0.061) | | | | |
| $R^2$ | 0.514 | 0.694 | 0.685 | 0.724 | 0.497 | 0.773 | 0.423 | 0.758 |
| Adjusted $R^2$ | 0.449 | 0.651 | 0.641 | 0.684 | 0.429 | 0.742 | 0.346 | 0.725 |
| $\Delta F$ | 7.894*** | 16.420*** | 15.349*** | 18.461*** | 7.370*** | 24.755*** | 5.484*** | 22.751*** |

* $p < 0.1$; ** $p < 0.05$; *** $p < 0.01$. Standard error in parentheses.

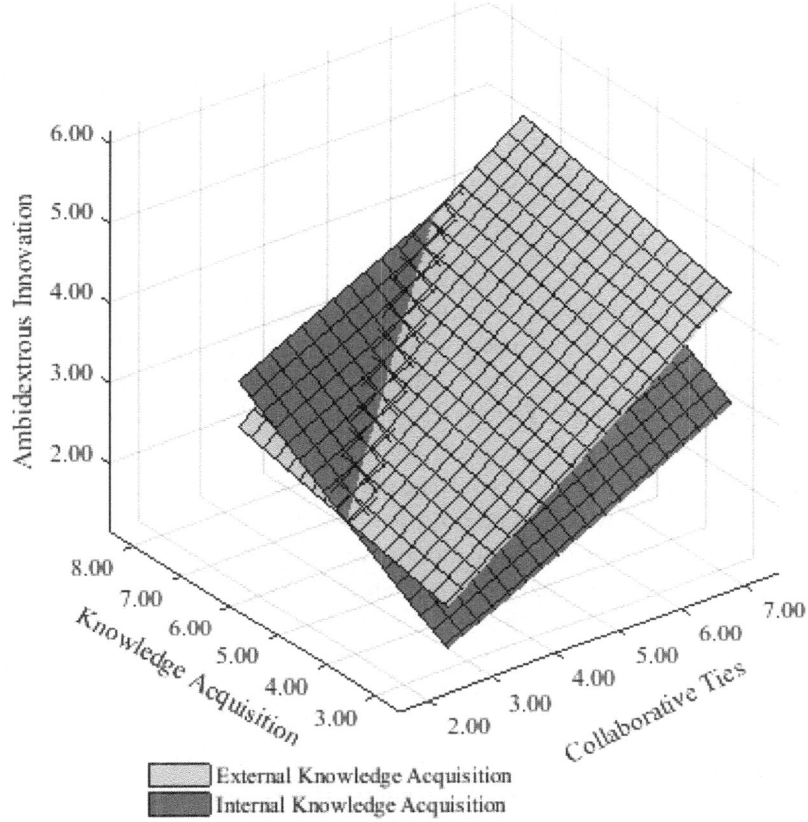


**Figure 2.** A 3-D graph for the comparison of the mediating effects of external knowledge acquisition and internal knowledge acquisition on the relationship between collaborative ties and ambidextrous innovation.

internal knowledge acquisition ($b$ = 0.275; 95% bias-corrected CI: [0.189, 0.374]). Thus, Hypothesis 3 is further supported.

In addition, to further exclude a multicollinearity concern, we estimated the variance inflation factors (VIFs). The results show that the VIFs' values ranged from 1.267 to 4.411, which were below the threshold value of 10. In addition, the results reveal that the tolerance levels were all greater than the threshold value of 0.10. Therefore, we found that multicollinearity was not a problem in our model.

## 5. Discussion and conclusions

Building collaborative ties has become an important strategy for firms to improve their ambidextrous innovation activities in transitional economies (Li et al. 2013). As little previous research had examined this topic, we wanted to investigate the relationship between collaborative ties and ambidextrous innovation with a focus on the mediating effect of knowledge acquisition. To do so, we used data from 323 firms existing in the transitional economy of China. We found that collaborative ties among partners had a

**Table 5.** Results of mediation analyses based on bootstrap method.

| | Indirect effects | | | |
|---|---|---|---|---|
| | | | Boot 95% confidence interval | |
| Mediators | Effect | Boot standard error | LLCI | ULCI |
| External knowledge acquisition | 0.097 | 0.055 | 0.007 | 0.205 |
| Internal knowledge acquisition | 0.275 | 0.045 | 0.189 | 0.374 |

Bootstrap resample = 5000. LLCI = Lower limit confidence interval; ULCI = Upper limit confidence interval; Estimates were calculated using the PROCESS macro.

positive effect on firms' ambidextrous innovation. As collaborative ties with different partners have positive effects on companies' innovation capability (Tomlinson and Fai 2013), we see that it is beneficial for the companies to conduct ambidextrous innovation activities (Guan and Liu 2016). Therefore, building close collaborative ties can be seen as a vital approach for firms to accelerate their innovation activities (Tomlinson 2010). We also found that collaborative ties among partners were more beneficial to the firm's external knowledge acquisition than internal knowledge acquisition. As knowledge sharing is a major characteristic of collaboration among partners, building collaborative ties among partner firms should be considered an essential manner for knowledge acquisition (Ahuja 2000). Given that collaborative ties can combine different external knowledge and promote the sharing of partners' knowledge (He, Ghobadian, and Gallear 2013; Wang 2016), close collaborative ties may be more beneficial to the firm's external knowledge acquisition than internal knowledge acquisition.

In addition, we found that knowledge acquisition mediated the relationship between collaborative ties and ambidextrous innovation, and the mediating effect of internal knowledge acquisition on this relationship was higher than that of external knowledge acquisition. Because knowledge is the core resource for firms to maintain a competitive advantage, the combination of internal and external knowledge resources is valuable for firms (Grimpe and Kaiser 2010); the acquisition of the two types of knowledge contributes to the promotion of companies' innovative capabilities (Grant 1996; Yam et al. 2011). In this regards, collaborative ties provide various sources (e.g. suppliers, customers, and competitors) for firms to acquire necessary knowledge, thus improving their innovation activities (Lee and Yang 2014; Shazi, Gillespie, and Steen 2015). Moreover, given that the internal knowledge acquisition is beneficial for facilitating knowledge mobility and the sharing of information among departments and individuals within a firm, the internal knowledge acquisition can help firms to incorporate external knowledge from collaborative ties into firms' ambidextrous innovation process better than that of external knowledge acquisition.

Overall, it is clear that collaborative ties, knowledge acquisition, and the ambidextrous innovation of firms are closely bound up with one another. Our findings remind us of the dynamic adoption of different types of knowledge acquisition and ambidextrous innovation modes to achieve better performance (Stock, Six, and Zacharias 2013; Venkatraman 1989).

### 5.1. Theoretical contributions

This study examined the effect of firms' collaborative ties on their ambidextrous innovation, and explored how knowledge acquisition affects the relationship between collaborative ties and ambidextrous innovation, thus offering insight into two significant areas.

Our work contributes to the literature on ambidexterity theory by revealing that collaborative ties are critical factors for the implementation of companies' ambidextrous innovation activities. Much previous research work has investigated the influences of exploratory and exploitative innovation on firms' development and growth (e.g. Hernández-Espallardo, Sánchez-Pérez, and Segovia-López 2011; Wei et al. 2014); however, little of that research discussed antecedent variables that may influence businesses' ambidextrous innovation activities. In this study, we filled this research gap from the perspective of collaborative ties, and verified the positive impact of firms' collaborative ties on their ambidextrous innovation. This work extends research on ambidexterity theory within a collaborative network framework.

Another contribution lies in the inclusion of knowledge acquisition as a key interceding mechanism to bridge the gaps in the collaborative ties–ambidextrous innovation relationship, which provides most of the explanatory power of ambidextrous innovation. On the one hand, this study extends the current literature by dividing knowledge acquisition into the categories of internal knowledge acquisition and external knowledge acquisition (Frenz and Ietto-Gillies 2009). Compared with prior studies that divided knowledge acquisition by various knowledge types, we separated knowledge acquisition by the different knowledge sources (Frenz and Ietto-Gillies 2009). On the other hand, we verified that both internal and external knowledge acquisition had mediating effects on the relationship between collaborative ties and ambidextrous innovation. As little consideration has been given to the effects of knowledge acquisition on the relationship between collaborative ties and ambidextrous innovation (Hernández-Espallardo, Sánchez-Pérez, and Segovia-López 2011), this paper extends our understanding of the importance of the integration of internal and external knowledge acquisition in collaborative relationships, and enriches knowledge management literature within the collaborative ties framework.

### 5.2. Managerial implications

As the acquisition of knowledge and the implementation of ambidextrous innovation activities are increasingly important for firms in the current competitive environment, our findings have some important implications for managers in terms of knowledge and innovation management. Our results suggest that building collaborative ties is the foundation of knowledge acquisition, and that knowledge is one essential lever for innovation (Isaksson, Simeth, and Seifert 2016). From a managerial standpoint, we argue that establishing close collaborative ties among partners and effectively leveraging the relationship between internal and external knowledge acquisition have enormous benefits for companies' ambidextrous innovation activities.

First, companies should establish collaborative networks to promote frequent communication between firms and amongst their partners. Our findings provide managers with evidence regarding the importance of collaborative ties. We argue that close collaborative ties are more beneficial for firms to carry out ambidextrous innovation activities (Guan and Liu 2016; Tomlinson 2010), and, therefore, companies need to build stronger collaborative networks to enhance close links with different partners. Moreover, given the potential negative effects of 'over-embeddedness' of high reliance upon collaboration partners (Tomlinson and Fai 2016), companies should cultivate their network management capabilities accordingly (Rampersad, Quester, and Troshani 2010).

Second, firms should pay more attention to ambidextrous innovation. As the implementation of ambidextrous innovation activities has a positive effect on a business' performance and growth (He and Wong 2004; Jansen, Van Den Bosch, and Volberda 2006), the sound adoption of the two modes of ambidextrous innovation can yield great benefits for that business. In addition, according to contingency theory (Stock, Six, and Zacharias 2013; Venkatraman 1989), the adoption of exploratory and exploitative innovation needs to be dynamically adjusted according to a business' particular stage of development in order to achieve better performance.

Third, firms should better integrate their acquired external knowledge with internal knowledge. As a single firm many have difficulties surviving in the current market, businesses need to collaborate with various partners to acquire knowledge (He, Ghobadian, and Gallear 2013). From the perspective of knowledge management, the transferring and sharing of knowledge are vital channels for knowledge acquisition (Filieri et al. 2014; Purchase, Olaru, and Denize 2014). However, it is a challenge for managers to turn their company's acquired knowledge into internal competencies for innovation, as knowledge that derives from different firms is harder to transfer (Dingler and Enkel 2016; Kogut and Zander 1992). Thus, businesses should pay more attention to the combination of internal and external knowledge to facilitate knowledge transfer across companies in order to take full advantage of innovation processes (Denicolai, Ramirez, and Tidd 2016; Dingler and Enkel 2016). In addition, as no single strategy works for every business, and no business can adopt a single strategy when its knowledge base accumulates over time (Lin and Wu 2010), managers should evaluate the knowledge assets of their firms and then deploy their innovation strategies accordingly.

### *5.3. Limitations and further research*

There are certain limitations to this study that could be explored in future research. First, this study was limited to a sample of Chinese manufacturing firms in the Yangtze Delta area, so there may be a concern that the results are both industry-specific and country-specific. Further study is encouraged to expand the range of the sample so that there will be greater generalizability. Second, this research which focus on the bright-side of collaboration ties for innovation may ignore the related problems associated with 'over-embeddedness' in collaboration (Tomlinson and Fai 2016). Thus, future research needs to explore the topic further from both the dark-side of collaboration. Third, this study only examined the mediating role of knowledge acquisition in the relationship between collaborative ties and ambidextrous innovation; it would be beneficial to explore other mediators that might affect the relationship in our model, such as firms' absorptive capacity and R&D capabilities. Nonetheless, this work leads us to believe that this study still yields new insights by examining the underlying relationship between collaborative ties and ambidextrous innovation in transitional economy. We also believe that the possible generalization of our findings to other economies is an interesting avenue to pursue in future research.

## Acknowledgments

This research was supported by the National Natural Science Foundation of China (Grant number: 71472118; 71772118; 71573185), Shanghai Pujiang Program (Grant number: 18PJC056), and Program for Professor of Special Appointment (Eastern Scholar) at Shanghai Institutions of Higher Learning.

## Disclosure statement

No potential conflict of interest was reported by the authors.

## Funding

This research was supported by the National Natural Science Foundation of China (Grant number: 71472118; 71772118; 71573185), Shanghai Pujiang Program (Grant number: 18PJC056), and Program for Professor of Special Appointment (Eastern Scholar) at Shanghai Institutions of Higher Learning.

## References

Agostini, L., A. Nosella, and R. Filippini. 2016. "Towards an Integrated View of the Ambidextrous Organization: A Second-Order Factor Model." *Creativity and Innovation Management* 25 (1): 129–141. doi:10.1111/caim.12167.

Ahuja, G. 2000. "Collaboration Networks, Structural Holes, and Innovation: A Longitudinal Study." *Administrative Science Quarterly* 45 (3): 425–455. doi:10.2307/2667105.

Armstrong, J. S., and T. S. Overton. 1977. "Estimating Non-Response Bias in Mail Surveys." *Journal of Marketing Research* 14 (3): 396–402. doi:10.1177/002224377701400320.

Atuahene-Gima, K. 2005. "Resolving the Capability—Rigidity Paradox in New Product Innovation." *Journal of Marketing* 69 (4): 61–83. doi:10.1509/jmkg.2005.69.4.61.

Baron, R. M., and D. A. Kenny. 1986. "The Moderator–Mediator Variable Distinction in Social Psychological Research: Conceptual, Strategic, and Statistical Considerations." *Journal of Personality and Social Psychology* 51 (6): 1173–1182. doi:10.1037/0022-3514.51.6.1173.

Bierly, I. I. I., E., . F. Damanpour, and M. D. Santoro. 2009. "The Application of External Knowledge: Organizational Conditions for Exploration and Exploitation." *Journal of Management Studies* 46 (3): 481–509. doi:10.1111/j.1467-6486.2009.00829.x.

Cao, Q., E. Gedajlovic, and H. Zhang. 2009. "Unpacking Organizational Ambidexterity: Dimensions, Contingencies, and Synergistic Effects." *Organization Science* 20 (4): 781–796. doi:10.1287/orsc.1090.0426.

Cassiman, B., and R. Veugelers. 2006. "In Search of Complementarity in Innovation Strategy: Internal R&D and External Knowledge Acquisition." *Management Science* 52 (1): 68–82. doi:10.1287/mnsc.1050.0470.

Chang, J., X. Bai, and J. J. Li. 2015. "The Influence of Leadership on Product and Process Innovations in China: The Contingent Role of Knowledge Acquisition Capability." *Industrial Marketing Management* 50: 18–29. doi:10.1016/j.indmarman.2015.04.014.

Chen, C. J., and J. W. Huang. 2009. "Strategic Human Resource Practices and Innovation Performance - the Mediating Role of Knowledge Management Capacity." *Journal of Business Research* 62 (1): 104–114. doi:10.1016/j.jbusres.2007.11.016.

Chen, P. L., and D. Tan. 2016. "Foreign Knowledge Acquisition through Inter-Firm Collaboration and Recruitment: Implications for Domestic Growth of Emerging Market Firms." *International Business Review* 25 (1): 221–232. doi:10.1016/j.ibusrev.2015.01.009.

Cohen, J., P. Cohen, S. G. West, and L. S. Aiken. 2003. *Applied Multiple Regression/Correlation Analysis for the Behavioral Sciences*. Mahwah, NJ: Lawrence Erlbaum Associates Publishers..

Cohen, W. M., and D. A. Levinthal. 1990. "Absorptive Capacity: A New Perspective on Learning and Innovation." *Administrative Science Quarterly* 35 (1): 128–152. doi:10.2307/2393553.

Demirkan, I., and S. Demirkan. 2012. "Network Characteristics and Patenting in Biotechnology, 1990-2006." *Journal of Management* 38 (6): 1892–1927. doi:10.1177/0149206311408319.

Denicolai, S., M. Ramirez, and J. Tidd. 2016. "Overcoming the False Dichotomy between Internal R&D and External Knowledge Acquisition: Absorptive Capacity Dynamics over Time." *Technological Forecasting and Social Change* 104: 57–65. doi:10.1016/j.techfore.2015.11.025.

Dingler, A., and E. Enkel. 2016. "Socialization and Innovation: Insights from Collaboration across Industry Boundaries." *Technological Forecasting and Social Change* 109: 50–60. doi:10.1016/j.techfore.2016.05.017.

Duncan, R. B. 1976. "The Ambidextrous Organization: Designing Dual Structures for Innovation." *The Management of Organization Design* 1: 167–188.

Dunlap, D., E. F. McDonough, R. Mudambi, and T. Swift. 2016. "Making up Is Hard to Do: Knowledge Acquisition Strategies and the Nature of New Product Innovation." *Journal of Product Innovation Management* 33 (4): 472–491. doi:10.1111/jpim.12298.

Edwards, J. R., and L. S. Lambert. 2007. "Methods for Integrating Moderation and Mediation: A General Analytical Framework Using Moderated Path Analysis." *Psychological Methods* 12 (1): 1–22. doi:10.1037/1082-989X.12.1.1.

Enkel, E., and O. Gassmann. 2010. "Creative Imitation: Exploring the Case of Cross-Industry Innovation." *R&D Management* 40 (3): 256–270. doi:10.1111/j.1467-9310.2010.00591.x.

Estrada, I., D. Faems, and P. Faria. 2016. "Coopetition and Product Innovation Performance: The Role of Internal Knowledge Sharing Mechanisms and Formal Knowledge Protection Mechanisms." *Industrial Marketing Management* 53: 56–65. doi:10.1016/j.indmarman.2015.11.013.

Filieri, R., R. C. McNally, M. O' Dwyer, and L. O' Malley. 2014. "Structural Social Capital Evolution and Knowledge Transfer: Evidence from an Irish Pharmaceutical Network." *Industrial Marketing Management* 43 (3): 429–440. doi:10.1016/j.indmarman.2013.12.011.

Forés, B., and C. Camisón. 2016. "Does Incremental and Radical Innovation Performance Depend on Different Types of Knowledge Accumulation Capabilities and Organizational Size?" *Journal of Business Research* 69 (2): 831–848. doi:10.1016/j.jbusres.2015.07.006.

Fornell, C., and D. F. Larcker. 1981. "Evaluating Structural Equation Models with Unobservable Variables and Measurement Error." *Journal of Marketing Research* 18 (3): 39–50. doi:10.1177/002224378101800104.

Frankort, H. T. W. 2016. "When Does Knowledge Acquisition in R&D Alliances Increase New Product Development? the Moderating Roles of Technological Relatedness and Product-Market Competition." *Research Policy* 45 (1): 291–302. doi:10.1016/j.respol.2015.10.007.

Frenz, M., and G. Ietto-Gillies. 2009. "The Impact on Innovation Performance of Different Sources of Knowledge: Evidence from the UK Community Innovation Survey." *Research Policy* 38 (7): 1125–1135. doi:10.1016/j.respol.2009.05.002.

Gilsing, V., and B. Nooteboom. 2005. "Density and Strength of Ties in Innovation Networks: An Analysis of Multimedia and Biotechnology." *European Management Review* 2 (3): 179–197. doi:10.1057/palgrave.emr.1500041.

Grant, R. M. 1996. "Toward a Knowledge-Based Theory of the Firm." *Strategic Management Journal* 17 (S2): 109–122. doi:10.1002/smj.4250171110.

Grant, R. M., and C. Baden-Fuller. 2004. "A Knowledge Accessing Theory of Strategic Alliances." *Journal of Management Studies* 41 (1): 61–84. doi:10.1111/j.1467-6486.2004.00421.x.

Grimpe, C., and U. Kaiser. 2010. "Balancing Internal and External Knowledge Acquisition: The Gains and Pains from R&D Outsourcing." *Journal of Management Studies* 47 (8): 1483–1509. doi:10.1111/j.1467-6486.2010.00946.x.

Guan, J. C., and N. Liu. 2016. "Exploitative and Exploratory Innovations in Knowledge Network and Collaboration Network: A Patent Analysis in the Technological Field of Nano-Energy." *Research Policy* 45 (1): 97–112. doi:10.1016/j.respol.2015.08.002.

Gupta, A. K., and V. Govindarajan. 2000. "Knowledge Flows within Multinational Corporations." *Strategic Management Journal* 21 (4): 473–496. doi:10.1002/(ISSN)1097-0266.

He, Q., A. Ghobadian, and D. Gallear. 2013. "Knowledge Acquisition in Supply Chain Partnerships: The Role of Power." *International Journal of Production Economics* 141 (2): 605–618. doi:10.1016/j.ijpe.2012.09.019.

He, Z. L., and P. K. Wong. 2004. "Exploration and Exploitation: An Empirical Test of the Ambidexterity Hypothesis." *Organization Science* 15 (4): 481–494. doi:10.1287/orsc.1040.0078.

Hernández-Espallardo, M., M. Sánchez-Pérez, and C. Segovia-López. 2011. "Exploitation-And Exploration-Based Innovations: The Role of Knowledge in Inter-Firm Relationships with Distributors." *Technovation* 31 (5–6): 203–215. doi:10.1016/j.technovation.2011.01.007.

Hung, K. P., and C. Chou. 2013. "The Impact of Open Innovation on Firm Performance: The Moderating Effects of Internal R&D and Environmental Turbulence." *Technovation* 33 (10–11): 368–380. doi:10.1016/j.technovation.2013.06.006.

Im, G., and A. Rai. 2008. "Knowledge Sharing Ambidexterity in Long-Term Inter-Organizational Relationships." *Management Science* 54 (7): 1281–1296. doi:10.1287/mnsc.1080.0902.

Inemek, A., and P. Matthyssens. 2013. "The Impact of Buyer-Supplier Relationships on Supplier Innovativeness: An Empirical Study in Cross-Border Supply Networks." *Industrial Marketing Management* 42 (4): 580–594. doi:10.1016/j.indmarman.2012.10.011.

Isaksson, O. H. D., M. Simeth, and R. W. Seifert. 2016. "Knowledge Spillovers in the Supply Chain: Evidence from the High Tech Sectors." *Research Policy* 45 (3): 699–706. doi:10.1016/j.respol.2015.12.007.

Jansen, J. J. P., F. A. J. Van Den Bosch, and H. W. Volberda. 2006. "Exploratory Innovation, Exploitative Innovation, and Performance: Effects of Organizational Antecedents and Environmental Moderators." *Management Science* 52 (11): 1661–1674. doi:10.1287/mnsc.1060.0576.

Jean, R. J., and R. R. Sinkovics. 2010. "Relationship Learning and Performance Enhancement via Advanced Information Technology: The Case of Taiwanese Dragon Electronics Firms." *International Marketing Review* 27 (2): 200–222. doi:10.1108/02651331011037520.

Karamanos, A. G. 2012. "Leveraging Micro-And Macro-Structures of Embeddedness in Alliance Networks for Exploratory Innovation in Biotechnology." *R&D Management* 42 (1): 71–89.

Katila, R., and G. Ahuja. 2002. "Something Old, Something New: A Longitudinal Study of Search Behavior and New Product Introduction." *Academy of Management Journal* 45 (6): 1183–1194.

Kogut, B., and U. Zander. 1992. "Knowledge of the Firm, Combinative Capabilities, and the Replication of Technology." *Organization Science* 3 (3): 383–397. doi:10.1287/orsc.3.3.383.

Kong, E. 2015. "A Qualitative Analysis of Social Intelligence in Nonprofit Organizations: External Knowledge Acquisition for Human Capital Development, Organizational Learning and Innovation." *Knowledge Management Research & Practice* 13 (4): 463–474. doi:10.1057/kmrp.2013.63.

Kotlarsky, J., and I. Oshri. 2005. "Social Ties, Knowledge Sharing and Successful Collaboration in Globally Distributed System Development Projects." *European Journal of Information Systems* 14 (1): 37–48. doi:10.1057/palgrave.ejis.3000520.

Laursen, K., and A. Salter. 2006. "Open for Innovation: The Role of Openness in Explaining Innovation Performance among U.K. Manufacturing Firms." *Strategic Management Journal* 27 (2): 131–150. doi:10.1002/(ISSN)1097-0266.

Lavie, D., U. Stettner, and M. L. Tushman. 2010. "Exploration and Exploitation within and across Organizations." *The Academy of Management Annals* 4 (1): 109–155. doi:10.1080/19416521003691287.

Lee, Y. M., and C. Yang. 2014. "The Relationships among Network Ties, Organizational Agility, and Organizational Performance: A Study of the Flat Glass Industry in Taiwan." *Journal of Management & Organization* 20 (2): 206–226. doi:10.1017/jmo.2014.32.

Lenz-Cesar, F., and A. Heshmati. 2012. "An Econometric Approach to Identify Determinants of Collaboration for Innovation among Firms." *Applied Economics Letters* 19 (3): 227–235. doi:10.1080/13504851.2011.572836.

Li, Y., Z. Wei, J. Zhao, C. Zhang, and Y. Liu. 2013. "Ambidextrous Organizational Learning, Environmental Munificence and New Product Performance: Moderating Effect of Managerial Ties in China." *International Journal of Production Economics* 146 (1): 95–105. doi:10.1016/j.ijpe.2012.11.008.

Liao, S. H., C. C. Wu, D. C. Hu, and G. A. Tsuei. 2009. "Knowledge Acquisition, Absorptive Capacity, and Innovation Capability: An Empirical Study of Taiwan's Knowledge-Intensive Industries." *International Scholarly and Scientific Research & Innovation* 3 (5): 338–345.

Liao, Y., and E. Marsillac. 2015. "External Knowledge Acquisition and Innovation: The Role of Supply Chain Network-Oriented Flexibility and Organizational Awareness." *International Journal of Production Research* 53 (18): 1–19. doi:10.1080/00207543.2015.1008106.

Lin, B. W., and C. H. Wu. 2010. "How Does Knowledge Depth Moderate the Performance of Internal and External Knowledge Sourcing Strategies?" *Technovation* 30 (11–12): 582–589. doi:10.1016/j.technovation.2010.07.001.

Lin, H., S. Zeng, H. Liu, and C. Li. 2016. "How Do Intermediaries Drive Corporate Innovation? A Moderated Mediating Examination." *Journal of Business Research* 69 (11): 4831–4836. doi:10.1016/j.jbusres.2016.04.039.

López-Sáez, P., J. E. Navas-López, G. Martín-de-Castro, and J. Cruz-González. 2010. "External Knowledge Acquisition Processes in Knowledge-Intensive Clusters." *Journal of Knowledge Management* 14 (5): 690–707. doi:10.1108/13673271011074845.

Lubatkin, M. H., Z. Simsek, Y. Ling, and J. F. Veiga. 2006. "Ambidexterity and Performance in Small-To Medium-Sized Firms: The Pivotal Role of Top Management Team Behavioral Integration." *Journal of Management* 32 (5): 646–672. doi:10.1177/0149206306290712.

Ma, R., and Y. C. Huang. 2016. "Opportunity-Based Strategic Orientation, Knowledge Acquisition, and Entrepreneurial Alertness: The Perspective of the Global Sourcing Suppliers in China." *Journal of Small Business Management* 54 (3): 953–972. doi:10.1111/jsbm.12222.

March, J. G. 1991. "Exploration and Exploitation in Organizational Learning." *Organization Science* 2 (1): 71–87. doi:10.1287/orsc.2.1.71.

Marín-Idárraga, D. A., J. M. Hurtado González, and C. Cabello Medina. 2016. "The Antecedents of Exploitation-Exploration and Their Relationship with Innovation: A Study of Managers' Cognitive Maps." *Creativity and Innovation Management* 25 (1): 18–37. doi:10.1111/caim.12139.

Martinez-Torres, R., and M. Olmedilla. 2016. "Identification of Innovation Solvers in Open Innovation Communities Using Swarm Intelligence." *Technological Forecasting and Social Change* 109: 15–24. doi:10.1016/j.techfore.2016.05.007.

Moorthy, S., and D. E. Polley. 2010. "Technological Knowledge Breadth and Depth: Performance Impacts." *Journal of Knowledge Management* 14 (3): 359–377. doi:10.1108/13673271011050102.

Park, B. I. 2010. "What Matters to Managerial Knowledge Acquisition in International Joint Ventures? High Knowledge Acquirers versus Low Knowledge Acquirers." *Asia Pacific Journal of Management* 27 (1): 55–79. doi:10.1007/s10490-008-9111-6.

Parker, H. 2012. "Knowledge Acquisition and Leakage in Inter-Firm Relationships Involving New Technology-Based Firms." *Management Decision* 50 (9): 1618–1633. doi:10.1108/00251741211266714.

Parra-Requena, G., M. J. Ruiz-Ortega, P. M. García-Villaverde, and J. Rodrigo-Alarcón. 2015. "The Mediating Role of Knowledge Acquisition on the Relationship between External Social Capital and Innovativeness." *European Management Review* 12 (3): 149–169. doi:10.1111/emre.2015.12.issue-3.

Podsakoff, P. M., S. B. MacKenzie, J. Y. Lee, and N. P. Podsakoff. 2003. "Common Method Biases in Behavioral Research: A Critical Review of the Literature and Recommended Remedies." *Journal of Applied Psychology* 88 (5): 879–903. doi:10.1037/0021-9010.88.5.879.

Preacher, K. J., and A. F. Hayes. 2008. "Asymptotic and Resampling Strategies for Assessing and Comparing Indirect Effects in Multiple Mediator Models." *Behavior Research Methods* 40 (3): 879–891.

Purchase, S., D. Olaru, and S. Denize. 2014. "Innovation Network Trajectories and Changes in Resource Bundles." *Industrial Marketing Management* 43 (3): 448–459. doi:10.1016/j.indmarman.2013.12.013.

Rabe-Hesketh, S., and A. Skrondal. 2006. "Multilevel Modelling of Complex Survey Data." *Journal of the Royal Statistical Society* 169 (4): 805–827. doi:10.1111/j.1467-985X.2006.00426.x.

Raisch, S., J. Birkinshaw, G. Probst, and M. L. Tushman. 2009. "Organizational Ambidexterity: Balancing Exploitation and Exploration for Sustained Performance." *Organization Science* 20 (4): 685–695. doi:10.1287/orsc.1090.0428.

Rampersad, G., P. Quester, and I. Troshani. 2010. "Managing Innovation Networks: Exploratory Evidence from ICT, Biotechnology and Nanotechnology Networks." *Industrial Marketing Management* 39 (5): 793–805. doi:10.1016/j.indmarman.2009.07.002.

Rosenkopf, L., and P. Almeida. 2003. "Overcoming Local Search through Alliances and Mobility." *Management Science* 49 (6): 751–766. doi:10.1287/mnsc.49.6.751.16026.

Rossi, F., A. Caloffi, and M. Russo. 2016. "Networked by Design: Can Policy Requirements Influence Organisations' Networking Behaviour?" *Technological Forecasting and Social Change* 105: 203–214. doi:10.1016/j.techfore.2016.01.004.

Rothaermel, F. T., and M. T. Alexandre. 2009. "Ambidexterity in Technology Sourcing: The Moderating Role of Absorptive Capacity." *Organization Science* 20 (4): 759–780. doi:10.1287/orsc.1080.0404.

Rubera, G., D. Chandrasekaran, and A. Ordanini. 2016. "Open Innovation, Product Portfolio Innovativeness and Firm Performance: The Dual Role of New Product Development Capabilities." *Journal of the Academy of Marketing Science* 44 (2): 166–184. doi:10.1007/s11747-014-0423-4.

Scott-Kennel, J., and A. Giroud. 2015. "MNEs and FSAs: Network Knowledge, Strategic Orientation and Performance." *Journal of World Business* 50 (1): 94–107. doi:10.1016/j.jwb.2014.02.004.

Sharif, N., E. Baark, and A. K. W. Lau. 2012. "Innovation Activities, Sources of Innovation and R&D Collaboration: Evidence from Firms in Hong Kong and Guangdong Province, China." *International Journal of Technology Management* 59 (3–4): 203–234. doi:10.1504/IJTM.2012.047244.

Shazi, R., N. Gillespie, and J. Steen. 2015. "Trust as a Predictor of Innovation Network Ties in Project Teams." *International Journal of Project Management* 33 (1): 81–91. doi:10.1016/j.ijproman.2014.06.001.

Stock, R. M., B. Six, and N. A. Zacharias. 2013. "Linking Multiple Layers of Innovation-Oriented Corporate Culture, Product Program Innovativeness, and Business Performance: A Contingency Approach." *Journal of the Academy of Marketing Science* 41 (3): 283–299. doi:10.1007/s11747-012-0306-5.

Sun, Y. 2016. "The Structure and Dynamics of Intra- and Inter-Regional Research Collaborative Networks: The Case of China (1985-2008)." *Technological Forecasting and Social Change* 108: 70–82. doi:10.1016/j.techfore.2016.04.017.

Tabachnick, B. G., and L. S. Fidell. 2007. *Using Multivariate Statistics*. Boston, MA: Pearson Education.

Tether, B. S. 2002. "Who Co-Operates for Innovation, and Why: An Empirical Analysis." *Research Policy* 31 (6): 947–967. doi:10.1016/S0048-7333(01)00172-X.

Tomlinson, P. R. 2010. "Co-Operative Ties and Innovation: Some New Evidence for UK Manufacturing." *Research Policy* 39 (6): 762–775. doi:10.1016/j.respol.2010.02.010.

Tomlinson, P. R., and F. M. Fai. 2013. "The Nature of SME Co-Operation and Innovation: A Multi-Scalar and Multi-Dimensional Analysis." *International Journal of Production Economics* 141 (1): 316–326. doi:10.1016/j.ijpe.2012.08.012.

Tomlinson, P. R., and F. M. Fai. 2016. "The Impact of Deep Vertical Supply Chain Relationships upon Focal-Firm Innovation Performance." *R&D Management* 46 (S1): 277–290. doi:10.1111/radm.12181.

Tushman, M. L., and C. A. O'Reilly. 1996. "Ambidextrous Organizations: Managing Evolutionary and Revolutionary Change." *California Management Review* 38 (4): 8–30. doi:10.2307/41165852.

Venkatraman, N. 1989. "The Concept of Fit in Strategy Research: Toward Verbal and Statistical Correspondence." *Academy of Management Review* 14 (1): 423–444. doi:10.5465/amr.1989.4279078.

Wang, C., S. Rodan, M. Fruin, and X. Xu. 2014. "Knowledge Networks, Collaboration Networks, and Exploratory Innovation." *Academy of Management Journal* 57 (2): 484–514. doi:10.5465/amj.2011.0917.

Wang, C. H., and L. C. Hsu. 2014. "Building Exploration and Exploitation in the High-Tech Industry: The Role of Relationship Learning." *Technological Forecasting and Social Change* 81: 331–340. doi:10.1016/j.techfore.2013.04.008.

Wang, J. 2016. "Knowledge Creation in Collaboration Networks: Effects of Tie Configuration." *Research Policy* 45 (1): 68–80. doi:10.1016/j.respol.2015.09.003.

Wei, Z. L., D. Yang, B. Sun, and M. Gu. 2014. "The Fit between Technological Innovation and Business Model Design for Firm Growth: Evidence from China." *R&D Management* 44 (3): 288–305. doi:10.1111/radm.12069.

Yam, R. C. M., W. Lo, E. P. Y. Tang, and A. K. W. Lau. 2011. "Analysis of Sources of Innovation, Technological Innovation Capabilities, and Performance: An Empirical Study of Hong Kong Manufacturing Industries." *Research Policy* 40 (3): 391–402. doi:10.1016/j.respol.2010.10.013.

Yang, J., J. Wang, C. W. Y. Wong, and K. H. Lai. 2008. "Relational Stability and Alliance Performance in Supply Chain." *Omega* 36 (4): 600–608. doi:10.1016/j.omega.2007.01.008.

Yli-Renko, H., E. Autio, and H. J. Sapizenza. 2001. "Social Capital, Knowledge Acquisition, and Knowledge Exploitation in Young Technology-Based Firms." *Strategic Management Journal* 22 (6–7): 587–613. doi:10.1002/smj.183.

Zack, M. H. 1999. "Managing Codified Knowledge." *Sloan Management Review* 40 (4): 45–58.

Zang, J., and Y. Li. 2017. "Technology Capabilities, Marketing Capabilities and Innovation Ambidexterity." *Technology Analysis & Strategic Management* 29 (1): 23–37. doi:10.1080/09537325.2016.1194972.

Zeng, S. X., X. M. Xie, and C. M. Tam. 2010. "Relationship between Cooperation Networks and Innovation Performance of SMEs." *Technovation* 30 (3): 181–194. doi:10.1016/j.technovation.2009.08.003.

Zhao, J. Y., X. Xi, and S. Yi. 2015. "Resource Allocation under a Strategic Alliance: How a Cooperative Network with Knowledge Flow Spurs Co-Evolution." *Knowledge-Based Systems* 89: 497–508. doi:10.1016/j.knosys.2015.08.016.

## Appendix

**Table A1.** Independent samples test.

| Variables | | Levene's test for equality of variances | | *t*-test for equality of means | | | | | | |
|---|---|---|---|---|---|---|---|---|---|---|
| | | | | | | | | | 95% confidence interval of the difference | |
| | | *F* | Sig. | *t* | *df* | Sig. (2-tailed) | Mean Difference | Std. Error Difference | Lower | Upper |
| Collaborative ties | Equal variances assumed | 0.089 | 0.765 | −0.816 | 160 | 0.416 | −0.130 | 0.159 | −0.444 | 0.184 |
| | Equal variances not assumed | | | | 159.894 | | | 0.159 | | |
| External knowledge acquisition | Equal variances assumed | 0.120 | 0.730 | −0.867 | 160 | 0.387 | −0.136 | 0.157 | −0.445 | 0.173 |
| | Equal variances not assumed | | | | 159.903 | | | 0.157 | | |
| Internal knowledge acquisition | Equal variances assumed | 0.520 | 0.472 | −0.595 | 160 | 0.553 | −0.099 | 0.166 | −0.427 | 0.229 |
| | Equal variances not assumed | | | | 159.042 | | | 0.166 | | |
| Exploratory innovation | Equal variances assumed | 0.530 | 0.468 | −0.643 | 160 | 0.521 | −0.120 | 0.187 | −0.490 | 0.249 |
| | Equal variances not assumed | | | | 159.663 | | | 0.187 | | |
| Exploitative innovation | Equal variances assumed | 0.530 | 0.468 | −0.557 | 160 | 0.579 | −0.083 | 0.150 | −0.379 | 0.212 |
| | Equal variances not assumed | | | | 159.829 | | | | | |

**Table A2.** Analysis of variance (ANOVA).

| Variables | | Sum of squares | *df* | Mean square | *F* | Sig. |
|---|---|---|---|---|---|---|
| Firm size | Between groups | 0.085 | 3 | 0.028 | 0.112 | 0.953 |
| | Within groups | 162.409 | 646 | 0.251 | | |
| | Total | 162.494 | 649 | | | |
| Industry sectors | Between groups | 0.403 | 26 | 0.016 | 0.060 | 1.000 |
| | Within groups | 162.091 | 623 | 0.260 | | |
| | Total | 162.494 | 649 | | | |

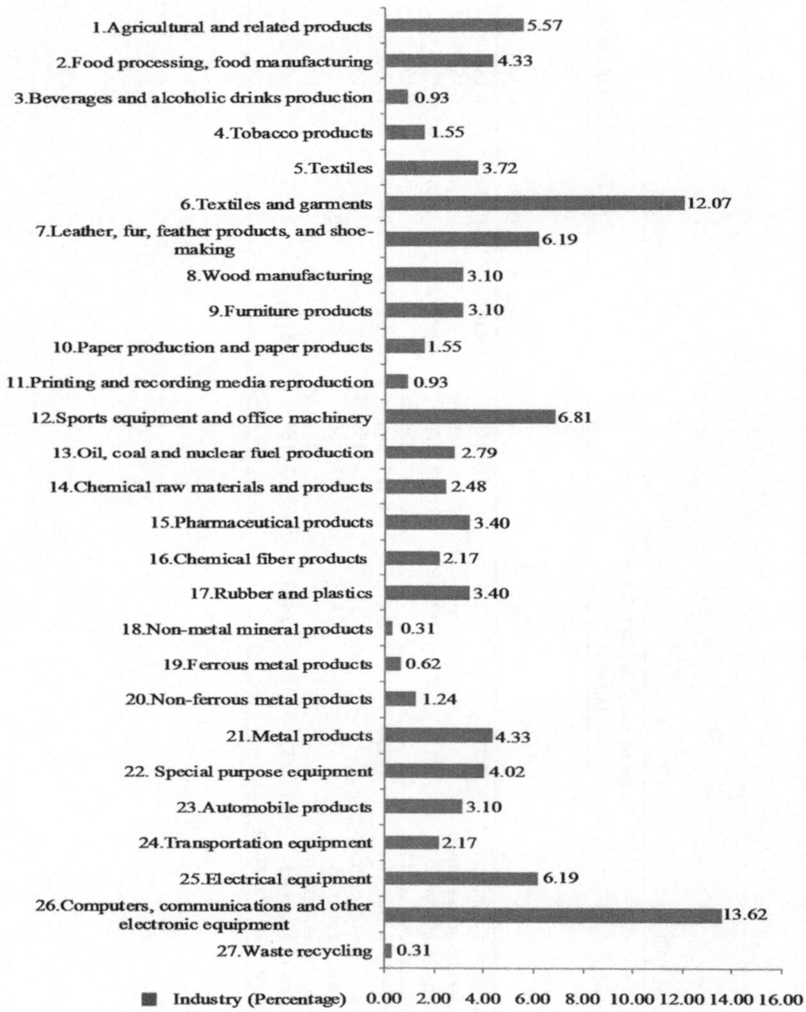


**Figure A1.** Industry distribution.

# Index


Acs, Z. 36
activities, open innovation 7–9, 11, 13, 16, 20, 23–24
adaptive capacity 2, 61, 64–68, 70, 75–77; harnessing 60–77; properties 64, 70, 76; theory of 68, 70, 75–76
Ahmed, P. K. 64
Ahn, J. M. 2
Alberti, F. G. 75
ambidexterity 81–83, 85
ambidextrous innovation 3, 81–85, 87–88, 90–91, 93, 95–99; activities 84–85, 87, 90–91, 95, 97–98; of firms 84, 96; modes 96, 98
Arrow, K. 37
Audretsch, D. 36

Baron, R. M. 91
Bentler, P. M. 16
Bogers, M. 11
Brazilian Institute of Geography and Statistics (IBGE) 33, 38–39, 50

Chandrasekaran, D. 90
Chen, C. J. 89
Chesbrough, H. 3
Chesbrough, Henry 35
Chiang, Y.-H. 8, 11
Chin, W. W. 15
Christensen, C. 34
climate 7–9, 11–12, 15–16, 20, 24
Cohen, W. M. 35, 64
collaboration breadth 13
collaboration depth 13, 20, 24
collaborative ties 81–99
competence trap 36
control variables 20, 42–44, 48–49, 90–91
cooperative ventures 33, 37, 49–50
Criscuolo, P. 3
Cronbach's alpha 15, 91
Cronholm, S. 69
cultural changes 2, 61–63, 72–73, 76; challenges 74–76

Damanpour, F. 8
data analysis 69
data collection 14, 68–69; procedures 14
De Marco, C. E. 62
D'Este, P. 38
Di Minin, A. 10
discriminant validity 16
Duncan, R. B. 81

econometric model 33, 49–50
Edwards, J. R. 93
Eisenhardt, K. M. 68
entrepreneurial orientation (EO) 9, 11, 13, 15–16, 20, 24
excessive economic risk 41, 43
exploitative innovation 82–85, 87–88, 90, 97–98; activities 3, 83, 87
exploratory innovation 82–83, 85, 88, 90
external information search breadth 13
external information search depth 13
external knowledge 2–3, 7–10, 13–14, 35–36, 48, 62, 82, 86–87, 91, 96, 98; acquisition 3, 81–82, 86–89, 91, 93, 95–97; exploration 9, 34–35, 49; sourcing 2–3, 38; utilisation in SMEs 6–24

Feldman, M. 36
financial obstacles (FINOBS) 33, 41–44, 48–50
Fornell-Larcker criterion 16
Frattini, F. 10
Freeman, C. 36
Fu, X. 10

Galia, F. 38
George, G. 10
Giddens, A. 65
Goldkuhl, G. 69
Granstrand, O. 11

Henseler, J. 15–16
Holgersson, M. 11
Hu, L. T. 16

Huang, J. W. 89
Hung, K.-P. 8, 11

importance–performance map analysis (IPMA) 7, 15, 20, 23–24
incentive 10–11, 13, 33
independent variables 16, 33, 41–42, 48–50, 88
indirect effects 37, 93, 96
innovation activities 2–3, 8, 32, 39, 41–42, 50, 70, 82, 96
innovation barriers 32, 37, 41
innovation management 97
innovation-oriented SMEs 14
innovation processes 2, 9, 35, 38, 60–63, 85, 88, 98
innovation strategies 32–33, 36, 63, 98
innovative ideas 82, 86
innovative SMEs 7, 23, 33
internal knowledge 38, 82, 91, 98; acquisition 3, 82, 86–88, 91, 93, 95–97; processes 3

Joint Open Labs (JOLs) 66–67, 73, 75

Kenny, D. A. 91
Khandwalla, P. N. 12–13
Kim, N. K. 2
knowledge acquisition 82–91, 95–98
knowledge exchanges 65
knowledge-intensive business services (KIBS) 33, 38–39, 42, 49–50
knowledge leak 75
knowledge management 2, 7, 9–11, 13, 23, 88, 98
knowledge management process (KMP) 13, 20
knowledge multiplexity 75
knowledge obstacles 2, 33, 37–38, 41, 43–44, 48–49; to innovation 38
knowledge sources 13, 32, 37, 84, 86, 97
knowledge transfer 75, 98

Lambert, L. S. 93
Laursen, K. 10–11, 13
Legros, D. 38
Levinthal, D. A. 35, 64
Li, Y. 90
loose coupling 2, 64–65, 70, 73–74, 76
Lucas, L. O. 2

Mahdad, M. 2
management practices 72–74, 76
March, J. 36, 82, 84
moderation effects 9, 21, 23
moderators 13, 15, 23
moderator variables 21
Moraes Silva, D. R. D. 2
multi-grounded theory approach 69
multiplexity 61, 64–65, 70, 75–77; of relationships 2, 72, 75

Naman, J. L. 12
Nelson, R. 37
new innovative companies 36

openness 2, 6–11, 13, 15, 23, 31, 34, 65; intensity 6–7, 10–11, 16, 23–24
Ordanini, A. 90
organisational efforts firms 7, 23
organisational facilitators 7, 10–11, 16, 23
organisational factors 11, 23–24
organisational flexibility (FLEX) 12, 15, 20
organisational moderators 6–24
organisational settings 8–9
ownership 90–91

Piccaluga, A. 10
PINTEC 33, 38–39, 49–50
Pizzurno, E. 75
policy implications 34, 49

questionnaires 69, 88

redundancy 61, 64–65, 70, 72–73, 75–77
Rentocchini, F. 38
research institutes 2, 32, 35, 41, 50
resource-based view (RBV) 7–8, 83, 85, 87
Ringle, C. M. 16
Rubera, G. 90

Salter, A. 3, 10–11, 13
sampling 14
Sarstedt, M. 16
Schumpeter, J. 34
7-point Likert scale 13–14, 89–90
Slevin, D. P. 12
small and medium-sized enterprises (SMEs) 2, 6–8, 11, 14, 21, 23–24, 32, 34, 37–39, 49–50
small entrepreneurial firms 36
Soete, L. 36
Staber, U. 64–65
structural model 16
structuration theory 65
survey questions 29–30
Sydow, J. 64–65

task redundancy 2, 73–75
technology-based SMEs 31–40, 42–44, 48–50; sample of 33, 42, 44, 48–49

Telecom Italia Group (TIM) 61, 66–67, 69, 76
Ter Wal, A. L. 3

universities and research institutes (URIs) 32–33, 36–38, 40–42, 48–50
university-industry collaboration 37, 49, 61, 66
university-industry cooperation 31–51

values 13–14, 16, 41, 61, 63, 91, 95
Vanhaverbeke, W. 3
variables 12, 20, 41–42, 48–50, 84, 90–91
Vega-Jurado, J. 38
Vonortas, N. S. 2

Wang, C. L. 64
West, J. 3

Xie, X. 2

Zahra, S. A. 10
Zang, J. 90
Zobel, A. K. 10
Zynga, A. 7